D0793562

Nature in Horsemanship

Nature in *Horsemanship*

Discovering Harmony through Principles of Aikido

Mark Rashid
Foreword by Crissi McDonald
Illustrations by Mike Theuer

Skyhorse Publishing

Copyright © 2011 by Mark Rashid

© 2011 Illustrations by Mike Theuer

All Rights Reserved. No part of this book may be reproduced in any manner without the express written consent of the publisher, except in the case of brief excerpts in critical reviews or articles. All inquiries should be addressed to Skyhorse Publishing, 307 West 36th Street, 11th Floor, New York, NY 10018.

Skyhorse Publishing books may be purchased in bulk at special discounts for sales promotion, corporate gifts, fund-raising, or educational purposes. Special editions can also be created to specifications. For details, contact the Special Sales Department, Skyhorse Publishing, 307 West 36th Street, 11th Floor, New York, NY 10018 or info@ skyhorsepublishing.com.

Skyhorse® and Skyhorse Publishing® are registered trademarks of Skyhorse Publishing, Inc.®, a Delaware corporation.

www.skyhorsepublishing.com

10 9 8 7 6 5 4 3 2 1

Rashid, Mark.
  Nature in horsemanship : discovering harmony through principles of aikido / Mark Rashid ; foreword by Crissi McDonald.
     p. cm.
  ISBN 978-1-61608-350-2 (alk. paper)
  1. Horses--Training. 2. Horses--Psychology. 3. Horses--Behavior. 4. Human-animal relationships. I. Title.
  SF287.R29 2011
  636.1'0835--dc23
                                2011014222

Printed in China

Contents

———————

Foreword

In addition to traveling to help people and horses around the country, Mark and I spend a fair amount of time studying to keep growing in our own knowledge and understanding. Our studies are not limited to horses, but certainly everything we have been learning can be applied to our work with them. The book you now hold in your hands is the result of Mark's many years of study in aikido, as well as current theories on animal behavior, brain anatomy and function, and many other topics.

For example, one of the things we have learned is that there is a theory about human brain function that states we actually have three brains, not just one. This theory states that nature doesn't throw away something that already works, so each part of our brain evolved around the previous part. Our first brain, what many know as our "reptilian brain," controls many of the bodily functions needed for survival: heart beat, breathing, etc. Our middle brain is very similar to the way many mammals' brains function, and in humans makes up the area where one of the processes is emotion. The last and uppermost part of our brain to develop, the neocortex (sometimes also referred to as the cerebral cortex), has evolved to be one of the biggest and most complex among mammals. Not only do we have three separate structures that are complexly connected, each brain has its own sense of time and space, its own way of seeing and remembering things, and its own way of processing incoming information.

What, you may be thinking, does this have to do with horses?

Although we spend most of our days using our higher brain functions for the tasks we perform, we also share many similarities with animals. We desire comfort, both in body and spirit. We make friendships and lasting bonds to not only those of our own species but outside our species as well. We like learning new things, enjoy having fun, and will seek out new experiences for their novelty. Through reading about the latest research on brain function, what I have come to understand is that as humans, we spend a great deal of our time in our third brain, the neocortex. One of the things this area of the brain does is take in millions of bits of information each day, process it all, and then put it all together in one big picture. There have been many studies done on how we think (you will read about "inattentional blindness" later on in this book) and what we see. We know that most people, most of the time, gather specific bits of information and process it into one big picture.

When we start looking at animals, however, they are almost opposite. Their brains are set up differently, and especially so in horses (or any prey animal). Horses, it turns out, are creatures of specificity. They see *everything*. Most horse owners can tell you about a time their horse spooked suddenly (to the person) and for no apparent reason. Or how the first three times their horse got in the trailer without any problems, but the fourth time the horse refused. The way we see things, and the way our brains process what we see, makes it almost impossible for us to spot changes in detail that horses can't help but see. I think the value in knowing this piece of information will greatly increase not only our understanding of horses but also our tolerance when they are alerted to something or, for some reason, act out of fear. It is about being able to step out of our own perspective and take what horses do far less personally. As I have often heard Mark say, horses aren't doing anything *to* us, they are just being horses.

It is our almost blind grip on thinking about everything that sometimes causes us to lose track of the horse itself. Going back to how our brains are set up, it is easy to see how automatic it is for us to gather information, sort it out, see the big picture, and make a decision based upon that. We all do it, every day, and don't really care how it happens, only that it does. To be realistic, this function is part of our species, and necessary not just for our survival but our growth as well. I think this is also why knowing a variety of techniques is important for a lot of horse people; we are using a part of our brains that we are really good at using, so there is a certain comfort in it. It is not as though technique is a bad thing, but what I am suggesting here is that it can be balanced with that part of ourselves that takes in information on a different level, the level horses live in. The part that we forget is that we don't necessarily have to think so much, so much of the time. I believe that one of the many reasons why we love being around horses—no matter what we have them for—is that they offer us an opportunity to experience something that is less about thinking and more about reconnecting with a wisdom that we don't often tap into. I have heard many people say they feel more grounded, more calm when they are around their horses. Masters of connecting, horses will give whatever they can of themselves, doing things that they normally wouldn't choose to do, because we ask. Perhaps remembering this when we are around these beautiful animals will help create a place where we can understand one another a little better, and fight a little less.

Within these pages Mark shares with us not only these ideas mentioned above, but also how we can potentially find a more harmonious way of working and being with our horses. He offers some unique and thought-provoking ideas on the nature of harmony, the rules of nature and the rules of man, and how nature has equipped all of us with not only the tools to survive but also many ways to grow. And how ultimately it is about honoring not only our place on this planet but every other creature as well.

All the best to you and your horses.

Crissi McDonald
Estes Park, CO
December 2010

Nature in Horsemanship

Chapter 1
Aikido and Horsemanship

———————————

"Don't challenge me," my aikido instructor said as he pushed me across the mat. Both the statement and the push took me by surprise. We were in the middle of a two-day aikido seminar, and my instructor had just finished demonstrating to the class a training technique in which he threw and then pinned me face-first on the mat. After releasing me, he effortlessly slid to one side and stood up. I stood up too.

At the time, I felt as though I was in pretty good shape for someone my age, especially considering the fact that I had been as careless with my body over the years as I had. I

was a *nidan*, second-degree black belt, and while still a long way from being able to do (or even *understand*) aikido with the effortlessness of the masters, I felt I could and had been holding my own during the seminar. Still, two four-hour days of aikido, which followed a full schedule of summer weeklong horsemanship clinics, had taken its toll on my already aching knees, shoulders, back, and elbows, and because of that, I thoughtlessly took the easiest path to get to my feet once released from the pin. Struggling, I had pushed myself up on my hands and knees and stood up, right in front of my instructor.

"Don't challenge me" was what I heard him say as he effortlessly shoved me nearly ten feet across the mat and over onto the hardwood floor. My immediate thought was that he had somehow misunderstood my intentions. All I had done was stand up, and challenging him hadn't even entered my mind.

Surely he had finished with me. After all, he had already turned and begun talking to the other students about the technique he had just demonstrated, and besides, I wasn't even looking at him, so how could he have possibly thought I was challenging him? Not only that, but I knew better than to challenge him in the first place. I had trained with this particular instructor a number of times over the years and had seen, and felt, firsthand, just how good he was.

While Sensei is *always* mindful of his *uke* (training partner, pronounced *oo-kay*), and always takes great care not to injure anybody, I have always felt I had yet to experience the full depth of what he was capable of. That coupled with knowing that my *ukemi* (pronounced *oo-kim-ee*, the art of defending one's self) was still sorely lacking in many areas, along with the fact that I was still only a few months into my recovery from reconstructive shoulder surgery, challenging him that day (or any other for that matter) wasn't even on my radar screen.

A squeak was heard as I left the mat, and my bare feet slid on the hardwood floor. "Don't challenge me," he repeated, before turning back to the students kneeling in a row next to the mat and continuing his explanation of the technique he had just demonstrated.

In the big scheme of things, it was nothing, a blip, a hiccup. The whole episode, from the time I stood up till the time I was standing on the hardwood floor, took less than two seconds. One would think something so inconsequential would be easy enough to brush off, and I suppose normally it would. But it wasn't. Not on that day, and not for me.

———

Even before I began *physically* training in aikido, I had already begun studying the art in other ways. For a couple years prior to ever entering a dojo, I read as many books and watched as many videos as I could about the techniques, principles, and most importantly, about the philosophy of the art. There were a number of ideas about aikido that immediately resonated with me, not the least of which were the focus on softness when entering into a conflict, blending and directing the conflict to the most peaceful solution possible—which includes doing everything possible to make sure the attacker doesn't get hurt—and ideally all those things are done with an overall lack of ego that is encouraged in its participants. Not only had all these ideas fascinated me, but I had already been trying to find ways to integrate them into my life, not to mention my work with horses, long before even hearing about the art of aikido.

So when I first began *physically* training in the art, I had what I thought to be a relatively clear understanding of these principles. To me they seemed pretty straightforward and, overall, fairly black and white. In fact, I was so clear about the principles and how I wanted to learn them while training in aikido that even before beginning my first class, I had already made up my mind that these would be my primary focus for as long as my training would last. The custom of moving up through the ranks would take a backseat, and to be honest, was really of no real interest to me.

Of course, it would take me quite some time to figure out that my concept of these ideas and principles, the preconceived opinion I was entering into my physical training of aikido with, and the *actual* meanings of them as O Sensei, the founder of aikido, put them forth were two completely different things. As far as I was concerned, there was only one true, and I should probably add, very narrow definition of each. O Sensei's idea, as I understand it now, was much broader.

I must say, my opinion of how things should have been did not do me any great service in my early days of training, and in fact, it was still causing me trouble right up until I was pushed off the mat. The reason I say this is that I was so locked into my own way of seeing things that any time I was forced to hold my beliefs up to the light and take a good hard look at them, the experience would almost always set me back in one way or another.

It's easy for me today to look back on my years of training and see all of the instances where my preconceived concepts of principles, of which I now feel I lacked a true under-standing, not only caused trouble for me but may have also caused trouble for those I trained with. However, instead of going into detail about every instance when I think this may have occurred, I think it may be more helpful to focus on only two. The first is the push from Sensei, which we'll get back to. The second happened on the night I was being tested for my second-degree black belt.

The test was held during an evening seminar at our dojo in Estes Park in which a number of visiting aikido, karate, and hojutsu instructors were present. While I had known about the seminar for some time, I had been on the road doing horsemanship clinics up until a couple days before the class was to be held, so although I knew about the seminar, I was unaware that testing was going to take place that night.

I was paired with another student from our aikido class for the evening. He was, at the time, already nidan and had been training in aikido as well as karate for many years. He was a masterful technician who had been one of my instructors ever since I first began training in aikido and a person for which I did, and still do, have a tremendous amount of respect.

The dojo was full of students from different martial arts disciplines that night, more than the six removable mats we normally used for aikido training would hold, so the decision was made to hold the seminar without the mats. Because we would be working on a hardwood floor, the head instructor, Shihan Scott, made a point to remind us all to be mindful and take care of one another during throws and pins so as not to injure each other needlessly.

With that, the seminar began. The first technique we were to perform was demonstrated by Mr. Scott and then was to be repeated by all of us students. It was a technique known as *nikkyo* we had all done many times before. This particular version began as uke grabbed *nage's* (the person performing the technique) lapel. Nage would then put uke in a wristlock in which the bones in uke's wrist are compressed. When done properly, nage has almost complete control over uke's body, and at that point, nage can take uke to the floor in a variety of manners. In this case, nage was to take uke to the floor by rolling uke's engaged elbow up toward his ear and then take him downward face-first, at which time nage could lock the entire arm out until uke would "tap out," a sign that the uke had reached the point of maximum flexibility of the joints involved. The tap is a universal sign that tells nage that the technique is not only effective, but also beginning to cause pain.

In this type of situation, it is customary that the higher-ranking student be the first to perform the technique, and the lower ranking student be the one acting as the "attacker." In this case I was the lower-ranking student, so after we bowed to each other (a sign of mutual respect in which I was offering my body for my partner to work with, and he in turn offers to take care of it) I then reached out to take hold of my partner's lapel.

What happened next would be just the beginning of the longest, and easily the most painful, evening of my life. The force and speed at which my partner applied the locks to my joints, as well as the force he used to take me to the hardwood floor was like nothing

7

I had ever experienced before. *KA-BAM!* Was the sound that echoed through the dojo as I slapped the hardwood floor with my hand in an attempt to lessen the impact of the fall. *KA-BAM!* Came the next fall and the fall after that and the fall after that, each one building greater in speed, intensity, and pain.

Within fifteen minutes from beginning the exercise, one of the visiting instructors, having seen and heard the force that my partner was using, came up and, with a knowing smile, said to him, "We're not trying to hurt anybody tonight." My partner bowed to him in acknowledgement, which I was relieved to see, feeling as though it might be the encouragement my partner would need to perhaps use a little less force and a little more finesse in his technique. We turned back to one another, bowed, and I reached for his lapel. *KA-BAM!* Down I went again, this time even harder than before.

After a while, Mr. Scott called the class to a halt so he could demonstrate another version of the technique, and shortly after that, I was once again crashing to the floor with all the force my partner could muster (or so it seemed to me). This went on for what seemed like the entire length of the seminar, which is why I was somewhat disheartened when I looked up at the clock to find that only forty-five minutes of the scheduled three hours had gone by.

My wrists, elbows, and shoulders already ached beyond belief from being locked out and stressed to the breaking point over and over, and my back, arms, hands, and hips were badly bruised from all the hard landings on the wooden floor. I knelt with all the other students next to the mat, catching my breath, as Mr. Scott demonstrated and then briefly discussed the next technique. When he motioned for us all to continue, I struggled to get to my feet as my now-swollen knees refused to take me to a standing position. Eventually I was up, faced my partner, and bowed. A second later, I hit the floor with yet another resounding *KA-BAM*, which echoed throughout the dojo.

Other than my partner getting a few more subtle, and even not-so-subtle, warnings throughout the evening from our instructors about taking it a little easier than he had been,

I actually remember very little else of the seminar. I don't remember any of the subsequent techniques we did, I don't remember anything that was said, and I don't have any idea how many times I was thrown and then got back up. In fact, the next thing I do remember about the evening was standing in line with the other students after the seminar was over and being called up to where our instructors were standing so that I could accept my promotion to second-degree black belt.

I had taken such a beating during the evening that by the time I got home, I was unable to lift my arms high enough to remove my *gi* (traditional training uniform), and my wife Crissi, who I needed to employ to help me remove the sweat soaked garment, was shocked to see the amount of bruising and abrasions that covered my body. It took nearly a month for me to physically recover from the seminar. It took even longer for me to recover from it emotionally.

———

Before going any further, I want to make it abundantly clear that I am not complaining about this particular seminar, nor am I complaining about the way my partner chose to train that evening. After all, aikido is a martial art, and anyone who gets into it thinking it's something less is in for disappointment. Training in martial arts is a lot like being around horses. Generally speaking, if you're into it long enough, it won't be a matter of *if* you're going to get hurt, it's a matter of *when*.

What I am talking about here is a situation that gave me a completely different perspective on how I not only look at aikido but also how I look at horsemanship and even life. What I had done that night in the seminar is what I think a lot of folks do with their horses. I turned the entire situation over to my partner, regardless of what the ultimate consequences might be, and then I wondered why I had taken such a beating for doing it.

Still, I didn't come to that conclusion right away. In fact, it would take nearly two months of difficult soul-searching before I could see that what had transpired that evening in the dojo was actually a major forward step in my learning, rather than just a first-class beating.

Admittedly, with my limited view of what I believed the principles of aikido to be at the time, it took me a while before I was able to look at the situation in a different light. During the days and weeks that followed the seminar, I seriously considered quitting aikido. I was really struggling with trying to reconcile what had happened that night with what I believed aikido could or should be. The only saving grace was that a few days after the seminar, I was scheduled to go back out on the road for a few months. Had I not gotten that break to completely step away from aikido, I'm not sure I'd still be training. But as it turned out, that break was just what I needed to get things worked out in my own mind.

The biggest problem I was having was that in the very beginning, the thing that drew me to aikido was the idea of developing harmony even during the most difficult of situations, and taking care not to injure an opponent even when they are attacking.

It had been very difficult, if not impossible, for me to see the harmony in what had happened during the seminar. I was simply unable to equate what I perceived as a general lack of regard for my physical well-being by my partner, someone who I thought should have known better, and the idea of blending and directing a conflict to the most peaceful solution possible.

Over and over, I played what I could recall of the seminar back in my mind, trying to find the good in what had happened. The only thing I could come up with was the weaker I got, the more power my partner seemed to have! Well, there's no question that might have been good thing for him. I wasn't real sure it was all that good for me.

But then more time passed, and as it did, the clearer and more in focus the picture began to get. I began seeing that I had been looking at the situation from a very one-sided perspective. All that time I had been trying to figure out why my partner chose to not harmonize with me. Why had he taken advantage of my weakened state to pummel me even more? Then it dawned on me. My partner hadn't taken advantage of me. He did his job.

He trained hard and with spirit. I, on the other hand, stood around and waited for him to change. I waited for him to see that I was having trouble and back off. In the meantime, I simply allowed him to continue to throw me hard, over and over, without changing a thing I was doing.

Aikido (much like horsemanship), by its very nature, is a highly personal art. It is all about improving one's self. But to achieve this improvement, the aikidoka enlists the help of training partners. These partners in turn are also working on their own aikido, their own personal improvement. The only way for harmony to be achieved while they practice together is if both individuals train honestly and to the best of their ability. This means that uke must give an honest attack, and nage must perform an honest technique. And in this honesty is where growth, and ultimately harmony, is achieved.

The night of the seminar, my partner had been performing honest technique. For a variety of reasons, I can see now that I had not been giving honest attacks, primarily in an attempt to get my partner to ease up. My ukemi had been rough and sloppy, partly because of my overall lack of physical flexibility and core strength, and partly because of lack of practice. As a result, my partner was doing his aikido to the best of his ability, but I wasn't doing my aikido to the best of mine. Because of that, true harmony was simply unachievable.

My partner refused to back off that night because then his best aikido would have been substandard and untrue to himself. In other words, he would have been doing my aikido, not his. By the same token, by allowing him to throw me around unchecked like I had, I had willingly given up my best aikido, and instead, I ended up only doing his aikido. I had sold myself short.

I see this happen all the time in the horsemanship clinics we do. The horse is always offering up the best of himself, whether it is the best turn or stop, the best forward, backward, or lateral movement, or even the best refusal, balk, or buck. The rider, on the other hand, often stops short of giving their best in return. They don't give an honest request or an honest correction, and sometimes, they don't even give the horse an honest ride. In many cases, the rider spends much of their time simply waiting for the horse to change their behavior so it fits the needs of the rider, even though the rider is stopping short of giving the horse the direction it needs to do so.

Just like me during the seminar, the riders sell themselves, and ultimately the relationship they have with their horse, short. As a result, true harmony with their horse is simply unachievable because when one individual gives their best and one doesn't, only discord and friction can result. The end result is that the rider often gives up his or her idea to the horse, and in doing so the horse begrudgingly takes control of the situation.

Coming to this clarification in my own mind allowed me to see that not only had I been doing my partner's aikido the night of the seminar, but in fact I had actually been doing his aikido ever since I first began working with him over ten years earlier. I realized that while I offered *my* aikido to all my other fellow students, when it came to that one person, I always gave up my aikido and ended up doing his instead.

I decided right then and there that that would change. Rather than quitting aikido, as I had been seriously considering right after the seminar, I found I was suddenly reenergized and couldn't wait to get back. Pulling into the dojo parking lot after a nearly two-month absence from class, something else suddenly dawned on me. In the past, anytime I came to class and saw my training partner's vehicle in the lot, I would get a small knot in my stomach. I hadn't even noticed it before. In fact, the only reason I noticed it that night wasn't because the knot *was* there, but rather because it *wasn't*.

I realize now that the knot I was experiencing whenever I saw my training partner's car in the parking lot is probably the same feeling many people get when they are around a horse they are struggling with. It's not necessarily a feeling of fear per se, but rather one of overall discourse, of something not being quite right. It's the absence of harmony, the absence of both individuals doing their best.

That night in class, and in every class since, I gave my partner nothing but my very best aikido.

———————

That brings us back to the seminar I spoke about earlier. Nearly two years had passed since the seminar in which I was promoted to nidan and the seminar in which I was unceremoniously pushed from the mat, and during that time I had done my best to offer up my best aikido to whomever I trained with. The two-day seminar had been no exception. As I previously mentioned, the push that Sensei had given me came after I had gotten up near where he was standing.

While my attacks and technique during the seminar had been the best I could give, I found by the second day I was feeling pretty fatigued. My knees and shoulders, which had always been a problem due to numerous injuries, were sore and aching, which seemed only to add to my fatigue. By the time Sensei had demonstrated that particular technique with me, I had nearly run out of steam. So instead of sweeping myself a safe distance away from Sensei after he let me go and springing to my feet as I had during the previous day's training, I pushed myself to my hands and knees and laboriously stood up right in front of him.

I believe any outsider looking in at the relatively helpless manner in which I made it to my feet would have been fairly certain I was in no way, shape, or form doing so as a challenge. So, as I mentioned earlier, I was surprised that Sensei would have seen it as one in the first place. But I guess more to the point, what really bothered me was I felt Sensei purposely took advantage of the relatively helpless state I was in to give me an unwarranted shove. This bothered me because if he had intentionally taken advantage of my situation, it would once again be in direct conflict with certain aikido principles, as I understood them at the time.

Aikido is primarily a defensive art, with its main purpose being to bring harmony to unharmonious situations and to do so as softly as possible and with an overall lack of ego.

I simply could not reconcile that with my perception of what had happened. I couldn't see how an instructor pushing an obviously helpless student constituted bringing harmony to an unharmonious situation. Not only that, but accusing someone of challenging you when it's obvious that they meant you no harm seemed a bit egotistical to me.

So these were the things I was struggling with as the two-hour morning session of the seminar came to a close. As we took our lunch break, I went home and mulled the situation over, although I'm sure most people wouldn't have given it a second thought. They would have simply made an adjustment if a similar situation came up by making sure to be clear of Sensei's "space" before they got up off the mat. But it just wasn't that simple for me.

The push Sensei gave me bothered me because it didn't fit neatly into my overall belief system of how I understood the principles of aikido to be. And that, it would turn out, would be the rub. Over the lunch break, I slowly came to the realization that there was really only one of two possible reasons why I was so troubled by the episode. Either Sensei had breached the principles of aikido by what he did, or my understanding of the principles was in some way flawed. It didn't take me very long to figure out that if something as trivial as what happened between us was bothering me so much, it probably had more to do with me than it did with Sensei, or even with what had happened.

I began looking at the situation with slightly different eyes. Part of my problem, it seemed, was that I had originally been looking at it as if I was a victim. I was thinking I was helpless because of my fatigue and because of the pain in my knees and shoulders. But I wasn't helpless. I was vulnerable for sure, but not helpless. Not only that, but I had put myself in that vulnerable position to begin with. It wasn't Sensei's responsibility to make sure I had enough energy in my tank to make it through the entire seminar. That was, and always had been, my responsibility.

I had fallen into the trap that I think a lot of people do when it comes to their health and fitness. I had become complacent with my physical situation. I had subconsciously talked myself into thinking that the way I was (knees, shoulders, and back being "bad") was just the way it was, and the way it was always going to be. Yet I hadn't taken the time, or made the effort, to try and change it.

This is something else we see all the time in horsemanship. People expect their horses to operate at a high physical level, whether it be going over that jump in perfect form, carrying itself in a collected frame for an extended period of time, running the perfect reining pattern, or even walking up and down the trails for hours on end. Yet many riders let their own bodies go. Sometimes this is just a symptom of growing older, sometimes it's due to old or new injuries, and sometimes it's due to lack of motivation. In fact, some (obviously not all) horse folks' only exercise throughout the day is mucking stalls and throwing hay over the fence. Some don't even do that. So while we expect physical excellence from the horse, we don't even come close to that for ourselves.

Admittedly, while I am certainly more physically active than a lot of people my age, what I had done is allow age and old injuries to dictate not only my overall range of motion but also my level of stamina. And while there wasn't really anything I could do about changing my actual chronological age, there were things I could and would do to improve my level of fitness so I didn't end up in a vulnerable position like the one I had found myself in at the seminar.

The second thing I came to realize was that, like the previous seminar I had taken part in nearly two years before, I, perhaps subconsciously, expected Sensei to "harmonize" with *me*. In other words, I expected him to take note of my physical condition and cut me some slack. While cutting someone slack is certainly a quality us humans find endearing, it isn't really found all that much in nature. Nature's harmony is all about survival of the fittest. Any animal of the same species crossing into another's territory, regardless of age or physical ability, is likely to be caught in a vigorous defense of the area by the individual that has already established the territory. It's as simple as that.

Harmony is all about balance, and for balance to be present or even achieved there must be some kind of order. A big part of that order is the individual self-protection of each animal within a species. By the individual protecting itself, it not only ensures its own survival, but it also ensures the survival of the entire species as well as any species with which it interacts. But I'll talk more about that later.

During the seminar, Sensei had maintained order by protecting himself. Whether I actually posed a threat to him that day or not didn't really matter. Real or perceived, any threat to that order must be quickly and effectively brought under control, which it had been. While the situation didn't seem particularly harmonious to me at the time, I can see now that it was absolutely congruent with the *development* of overall harmony. And it is the *development* of harmony that aikido, *and* horsemanship, is all about.

By the time we had come back to the dojo later that afternoon to finish the final two hours of the seminar, I had pretty much had all of that worked out in my head. It would take much longer before I truly understood it, however.

———————

I once read a quote that said, "When a religious theory is proven to be unfounded by science, then that theory must give way to science." Just as I'm sure people of deep religious faith might take issue with that statement, so I found I was taking issue with having my convictions about aikido turned upside down—not just once, but twice within just a few short few months of each other!

I had been absolutely certain that I understood the principles of aikido even before I began physically training in the art, and for many years I held on to those convictions like they were gold. The only problem, and what I would eventually come to understand, was that when a belief becomes stagnant, growth is not possible.

After these two seminars, I had a couple of choices about my own beliefs. I could either continue holding on to them as I had been, or I could take a long hard look at them and see if there was something more for me within them, perhaps something that I had been missing. What I found would not only change the way I look at aikido, but it would also have a profound change in the way I looked at and approached my horsemanship as well.

Chapter 2
Nature's Harmony

Things had been going smoothly all day. It was the last day of a four-day clinic, and I was feeling pretty good about the changes I had seen between all the horses and riders that had been in attendance. There had been no real problems to speak of, and overall, the entire clinic had been relatively uneventful. When the second to last horse and owner came into the round pen, I had no reason to think I would see anything different.

The horse was a six-year-old Tennessee Walker named Crockett that had been little more than a pasture ornament for the vast majority of its life. The owner, a nice middle-aged fellow named Jerry, was relatively new to horses but had always wanted to own one. When

a neighbor decided to sell this horse, Jerry snapped at the chance to buy him. He quickly found out, however, like so many other new horse owners, that watching horses from afar and having one in your own backyard are two very different things.

It didn't take Jerry long to see that Crockett had very little education when it came to knowing how to act when he was around people. He was dangerously aggressive at feeding time, wasn't a real big fan of allowing himself to be caught, and was extremely pushy while being led. Jerry also found that while the horse's behavior needed some work in order for him to be safe to be around, his own education when it came to knowing how to act around the horse needed work as well.

Jerry had enlisted the help of a cousin who owned horses to see if she could get Crockett's issues sorted out, and apparently she ended up with a broken wrist and dislocated shoulder for her trouble. He then took Crockett to a local trainer who, while avoiding any serious injury, had not had much luck altering the gelding's behavior either. After a few more trainers and a few more failed attempts, he was ready to sell the gelding and get out of horses altogether, but had decided to bring Crockett to the clinic as a sort of last-ditch effort to see if the pair's relationship could be salvaged.

At the time, I had been spending a great deal of my focus when working with troubled horses, keeping them just this side of trouble. What I mean by that is I felt if I could keep the horse in a thinking frame of mind instead of tripping them over into a panicked or defensive state of mind, that it would be easier for them to learn and thus easier for them to change any unwanted or undesirable behavior they may be carrying around.

This way of thinking was a source of several discussions between myself and a good friend of mine who was also a clinician. My friend was of a mind that sometimes, in order to get a change from a troubled horse, you needed to tap into that part of their brain where the fight in them lived so they could learn to work through the fight, rather than avoiding the fight altogether. I always thought this argument was a valid one, especially seeing how effective it had been during the times when I watched him work with troubled horses. He was always very direct and to the point with troubled horses, and even though the horse would get into a much more worried state of mind when he firms up with them, which often translated into very defensive behavior on the horse's part, the horse always got better. Most of the time it would get substantially better.

I, on the other hand, was trying to find a quieter way of doing things. Because of that, I had been working hard at keeping the horses I worked with out of that worried and defensive state of mind. For the most part I felt I had been pretty successful with the majority of the horses I worked with in this manner, including Crockett.

On the first day of working with him, I got the impression the gelding simply didn't know very much, and what he did know was not terribly helpful when it came to him being able to get along with people. Crockett was so pushy that I ended up having to go to the gelding's pen with Jerry on the first day just so I could help lead him to the round pen to work with him. The horse had no boundaries whatsoever and was intent on running Jerry over even before he got him out of the pen. I stepped in and explained to Crockett as quietly, but effectively, as I could that what he was doing was unacceptable behavior, and within about fifteen minutes, he had quieted down, and we had him in the round pen.

That first day, we spent the majority of Jerry's session teaching Jerry how to lead his horse and teaching Crockett how to follow, which he would do, albeit grudgingly. Having had very little in the way of meaningful guidance by humans during his life, it quickly became clear that not only did Crockett not know very much in the way of training, but he also didn't really even know how to learn. So after the leading lesson was finished, we spent much of Jerry's sessions over the next couple days teaching Crockett some simple things designed not only to get him in a learning state of mind but also to teach him how to turn some of his decision making over to Jerry.

On the second day, after checking in with the leading lesson from the previous day, which, while not going as well as I would have liked, was going better than it had been, we worked on teaching both Jerry and Crockett how to lunge properly. In doing this, I put Crockett on a long line and asked him to circle around me as I walked with him and helped him understand how to go forward, change speeds, and stop. Once he understood these three relatively simple tasks, I turned him over to Jerry, and Jerry repeated everything I had done with the gelding.

The next day we covered everything we had worked on with Crockett from the previous two days, and when I felt his leading and lunging looked pretty good, we started teaching the gelding how to ground drive. Ground driving is really nothing more than teaching the horse how to stop, turn, and back up with two long driving lines that are attached to the sides of his halter. Lunging and ground driving are two of the steps I use during the initial steps of starting colts as I find it helps them learn some relatively simple tasks which will not only serve them later in life, but also teach them how to turn their decision making over to someone else—which was a skill that Crockett needed pretty badly.

I would have to say that both Jerry and Crockett seemed about average as far as their skill in picking up the things we were trying to teach them, and Crockett also seemed relatively amenable during the whole process. I say *relatively* amenable because each time we began showing him a new task, he would protest by shaking his head or stomping his feet or acting out in some other way. Overall, however, even that was minor compared to the fit he originally pitched on the first day when I had to go help Jerry retrieve the gelding from his pen.

So when Jerry brought Crockett into the round pen on the last day, I had no reason to believe there was going to be any trouble between them. I was happy to watch as Jerry took his time working through the things we had done with Crocket there in the round pen during the previous three days. He first took some time lunging the big sorrel gelding, and when that all looked good, he hooked a second line on Crockett's halter and went to ground driving.

I realize that for some folks, teaching an owner how to do little more than lunge and ground drive his horse doesn't seem like much information to take home from a four-day clinic. But I wanted to give this particular pair something easy enough to do that they could both not only accomplish it, but that over time they could excel in it, and that would help build confidence in each other. Lunging and ground driving seemed to be the most logical choices at the time, and up until that last session, I felt we'd hit the nail right on the head. Crockett, it would turn out, had a completely different take on the matter.

The gelding did everything Jerry asked of him during that last session, although none of it seemed terribly soft, or even very willing. Still, by the time the session was over, Jerry had successfully covered leading, lunging, and ground driving without me having to go into the pen and help, which I had done during the previous three days. Jerry unhooked the two long cotton driving lines from Crockett's halter at the end of the session, and I went into the pen and took them from him so I could coil them up and put them back in my equipment bag.

Jerry walked over near the gate and was visiting with a couple of the auditors who had been watching, and I moved to where my bag lay, just outside the round pen fence. Crockett remained standing quietly in the middle of the pen. I pulled my bag under the bottom fence rail and into the pen and placed one of the lines in it then turned to see what, if anything, Crockett was doing. As I caught his eye, a strange feeling came over me that I couldn't quite put my finger on, so instead of placing the other coiled rope in the bag, I turned and watched him more carefully.

As if he had planned it, the big gelding looked at me then turned and looked at Jerry. He turned back and looked at me and then back at Jerry, then very deliberately he turned, walked over to where Jerry was standing and, without even breaking stride, walked right over the top of him. Having just nonchalantly stepped on Jerry's feet and pushed him hard into the fence, Crockett then turned and looked back at me. It was if he was saying, *You boys may think we're done for the day, but we aren't.*

"Well," I said as Jerry cleared himself out of the spot he was in. "We can't quit on that." And with that, I clipped a lead rope on Crockett's halter and we began to revisit some of the previous days' lessons on leading and boundaries. I quickly found, however, that Crockett wasn't very interested in working quietly, the way I would normally try to do. Each time I presented something I felt he already understood, he would respond by pitching some kind of fit, and the quieter I tried to get, the more he escalated until I simply had no choice but to defend myself in any way I saw fit—which I did. Even with that, I quickly realized that Crockett was mostly on the offensive, and I mostly on the defensive, which is no way to be working with a horse in almost any situation, and certainly not in this one.

Crockett had tapped into that part of the brain where his fight lived, and as much as I didn't want to go there, if I were to help him find a way to feel better, I would have to get in the middle of it and help him work through it—which I did. The next forty-five minutes were not pretty to watch. There was a lot of dust, a lot of lead rope swinging, a lot of pushing, pulling, rearing, running, jerking, squealing, foot stomping, and sweating. But by the time we had finished, there was a completely different horse standing there in the pen with me.

Having thrown everything he had into the mix during our forty-five minutes of animated discussion, Crockett had completely given up his desire to fight and finished the session by becoming very quiet, willing, and responsive, for both me and Jerry. Watching Jerry and Crockett heading quietly back to his pen following the ordeal, I came to realize I had learned a very important lesson. That lesson was that sometimes the human way of wanting to bring things into balance or harmony and nature's way of wanting to bring things into balance or harmony can be two very different things.

For the most part horses are very harmonious creatures and do whatever they can to get along with one another. In fact, once an order is established within a herd, that order usually remains unchanged for a very long period. However, if ever the time comes when a herd member's behavior in some way threatens the balance of the herd, another horse may feel the need to challenge or otherwise impose its will on that horse as a way to bring things within the herd back into balance. When this happens, it is usually done as a way to keep or improve the overall strength of the herd. Sometimes when this is done, an all-out fight might break out between the two horses in question whereas other times the matter might be settled by nothing more than a quick glance or the pinning of ears. It is nature's way of not only keeping the herd resilient but also in balance.

It is my belief that domestic horses also want nothing more than to be in balance, both within themselves and with us. It is for that reason that I think horses like Crockett, having been offered very little, if any, human direction or leadership during their life, suddenly act out the way they do when someone finally does offer them some leadership. I believe the reason for this "acting out" is that a domestic horse that has inadvertently been put in control of the vast majority of situations they get in when around humans often ends up developing a false sense of balance. With no one to follow, they become the leader by default, and when the human finally does step up and ask the horse to take some guidance instead of give it, the horse often sees the gesture as a challenge.

Much like that day during the seminar with Sensei, rather than waiting to see if the threat is real or not, a horse feeling challenged by someone might simply send out a warning push of some kind as a way to meet the "challenge." If that doesn't bring the "challenge" to an end, they will push harder, possibly triggering some kind of full engagement as a way to bring the issue to a conclusion, such as the one Crockett and I went through, until the matter eventually gets resolved one way or the other. Any unresolved issue in the horse world is a lack of balance. It's like anything else in nature. When things get far enough out of balance that critical mass is reached, then something pretty dramatic often happens before balance, or harmony, can be reachieved. This is nature's way of creating and maintaining harmony.

Now, while it was my work with horses and in ranching that helped me start heading toward that understanding, it was my work in aikido that would eventually help me *get* to that understanding. The word *aikido* itself can be loosely translated to mean "The Way of Harmony." When I first began training in the art, and even before, I believed the idea of "bringing harmony" referred to the fact that someone who trains in aikido would eventually attain the ability to bring resolution to dangerous physical situations by means of applying the martial aspect of the art to the situation. Or perhaps another way to say it would be that aikido is a way of bringing balance to an unbalanced state of affairs.

The longer I have trained and studied the art, however, the more I have begun to realize that while the martial aspect of aikido is most certainly an important part of the study, the bigger and broader sense of the art is actually much deeper. What I have come to understand is that aikido, like horsemanship, is very much an internal art that is practiced externally, and when harmony is lacking on the inside of a person (or horse), it will most certainly be lacking on the outside.

It should be pointed out here that when I use the word *harmony*, I am not using it in the relatively idealistic manner in which many folks, particularly in the horse world, use the word these days. To many people, the word *harmony* signifies the absence of strife, struggle, or confrontation. However, I believe that might be a somewhat narrow and relatively unrealistic view of the meaning of the word.

The truth of the matter is, harmony and confrontation are not mutually exclusive. In order to achieve harmony, there must first be some kind of inconsistency or divergence. We simply cannot have one without the other. It is the struggles and/or confrontations in nature that not only produce harmony, they also tend to create positive change and growth throughout an entire area, species, or number of species.

For example, predators in the wild prey on the weak, old, and sick. In turn, what is left is the young, strong, and fast, so in order for future generations of predator and prey to survive, both must become quicker, hardier, and more agile. This means the predators become better hunters, which causes the prey to become better at escaping, which improves both species. It is true harmony in action. Nature's harmony, which states that everything that is here on earth must in some way—whether directly or indirectly—be of benefit to *everything* else.

But predators and prey are only one example of nature's harmony. Examples can be found everywhere we look. Back before man's intervention, trees would slowly begin appearing in areas where only grass had been in the past. Overtime, those trees would take over the grassland, eventually turning it into a forest. Unmolested for a century or more, the trees would grow to an old age, and at some point lightning would strike and start a fire. The fire would spread, and thousands of acres of trees would be wiped out. Then the rains would come and extinguish the fire, leaving behind a charred landscape, which in time would again begin to turn green. But this time, it would be the ground-covering plants that would return, the ones that couldn't grow before due to the heavy canopy of tree branches blocking out the sun. The dead, burnt, and decaying trees then provided the nutrients for the soil that the new plants would need to grow. Grazing animals would return to the area where only tree dwellers had been, predators would follow the grazers, and another cycle of nature's harmony would begin.

And nothing in nature is immune to these ebbing cycles. Horses shed their coats of heavy winter hair, which is replaced with a lighter, thinner coat of summer hair. However, no sooner will the horse's summer coat have grown in than almost immediately the hair begins to shed once more, making way for the next season's heavy winter coat.

Even the sun itself goes through cycles of changes. According to hundreds of years of research, deep inside the sun, giant loops of magnetic forces are generated. These loops expand and eventually burst through the sun's surface, causing solar storms, which lead to a drop in temperature in that area that is seen as a dark blotch on the sun's surface. These blotches are referred to as sunspots, and the sunspots are very active for an eleven-year period. When the numbers of sunspots drop at the end of each eleven-year period, the solar storms die down, and all becomes much calmer. In scientific terms, this calming is referred to as a "solar minimum," and it doesn't last very long. Usually within a year, the spots and storms begin to build into what is referred to as the "solar maximum," and another eleven-year cycle begins. In order to maintain harmony within itself, even the sun must go through changes.

If we take this idea of nature's harmony one step further, one might even find that for every "problem" that develops here on earth, nature always provides a solution. For instance, in areas where biting bugs are prevalent, there will also be an abundance of plants that counteract the bites as well as birds and reptiles to eat the insects. Another example might be how in the Western United States where the evergreen forests had been recently allowed by man to grow much older than nature would normally allow, pine beetles showed up and killed the trees anyway, which makes way for the ground plants to begin to grow. And yet another example is how, as man evolved over the centuries and exotic diseases or other maladies developed, nature provided other humans with the capacity to find cures or treatments as well as all the materials necessary to develop the pertinent medicines and build equipment to deal with them.

Nature's way of dealing with things consists of a continuous cycle of give and take. If nature gives something, it takes something in return, and if it takes something, it also gives something in return. So unlike the way we humans might see the world around us, where everything must be fair and just and if it isn't someone must take the blame or be held accountable, nature, on the other hand, is all about balance. And in nature's way of balance, there is no good or bad or right or wrong, but rather there is only what is of benefit to the whole. Balance is nature's way of dealing with issues, and keeping that balance may not always be the quickest, most painless, most convenient, or even prettiest way for us here on earth, but it is *always* the right way.

———

Because we humans have a tendency to look at the world around us in terms of right or wrong in accordance with what we believe, understanding nature's harmony can at times be very difficult for us. For instance, it can be hard for us to watch a lioness stalk and kill a weanling zebra without judging the lion and feeling bad for the zebra. For many people, the lion would instantly become the "bad guy," and the zebra the poor victim.

Yet the meat the zebra provides will not only feed the lioness, but other members of her pride including her young. It will also feed the various scavengers of the plains, including birds and insects. What is left of the carcass when all are finished with it will nourish and fertilize the ground, which will help grow the grasses that the remainder of the zebra's herd will eventually feed on. In time, all the animals, birds, and insects that fed off the zebra will also die, and their carcasses will go to feed and nourish others in the same way the zebra fed and nourished them. So while the act of the kill may be uncomfortable for us to watch, the result of the kill actually benefits and helps bring life to all, including those not even born yet. Once again, it's nature's harmony in action.

Feeling bad about watching a predator kill its prey is a fairly typical human response to the situation. A human who is uncomfortable about something will often look for someone or something to blame for the way they feel long before they look for a way to feel better. An animal, on the other hand, will simply look for a way to feel better. Staying in balance, or getting back in balance once out, is way more important to an animal than trying to figure out the reason for the imbalance in the first place.

While the lioness was able to catch and kill one weanling zebra, the rest of the herd would be able to get away by fleeing in a sort of organized panic. Once they understood they were no longer in danger due to the weanling having been brought down (prey animals recognize that predators don't keep killing after they have already made a kill), they can then set to the business of "resetting" or regaining their emotional balance. They do this in a variety of ways which actually begins with them running from the threat, but then also includes regulating their breathing and going into a sort of uncontrollable shaking that gradually dissipates as the body regains its balance. Within a very short period of time fol-lowing the attack, the individuals within the herd will have rebalanced themselves, which allows the entire herd to get back in balance as a unit. Usually after between thirty minutes to an hour has passed, all will have quieted down and gone back to grazing.

Because of animals' inherent need to be in balance and stay in balance, a horse's way of searching for balance within himself and a human's way of trying to help an unbalanced horse may, and often does, look very different, such as in the case with Crockett. I had hoped I could help him feel better by being quiet and giving him some direction. He apparently didn't care how he got to feeling better, just that he did. My guess is the route he chose to get there was the shortest distance between two points, and even though it was harder on both of us than something perhaps a little quieter might have been, it was what *he* needed to have happen in order for him to bring himself back into balance.

I bring up this point about how nature brings things into balance and how humans often perceive it because when it comes to working with horses, we humans sometimes have a hard time doing what it takes to help a horse reach a balanced point (because it makes us feel uncomfortable) or watching a horse as it works to get itself into balance (also because it makes us uncomfortable).

Several years ago, I was using an older ranch gelding named Mouse to perform demonstrations at a clinic. I had purchased Mouse from a friend, and due to Mouse's previous rough handling (by the person who owned him before my friend got him), he could be more than a little worried around people he didn't know and was pretty reactive and defensive on the ground. For the most part, however, I had noticed he was usually a no-nonsense type of guy when he was working, with very little spooking or showing the type of worry under saddle I had seen with him on the ground.

My assistant at the time was using a young mare that I had raised named Dancer. We were at the end of a three-week-long travel schedule during which time Mouse and Dancer had lived together both in the trailer and in the corrals at the venues where we were clinicing. They had also lived in the herd together at home for over a year prior to taking this trip, and at no time during that year had either one showed a whole lot of interest in the other.

It was for that reason that I was somewhat surprised when, out of the blue, Mouse suddenly decided he and Dancer were married. On the second day of the last clinic of the trip, Mouse and I were working with a student out in the outdoor arena while my assistant and Dancer were working with another student over in the indoor arena. This was the exact same setup we had had the day before and Mouse had shown absolutely no signs of worry or concern for his traveling partner at that time. Yet on this day, he was suddenly beside himself. He couldn't stand still, he called endlessly, pawed the ground, shook his head, and kept looking back toward the indoor arena no matter what direction he was standing.

At lunchtime, Mouse was tied to the trailer next to Dancer. He stood quietly with his head down, and when I took him back out after lunch, the whole thing started over again. He appeared inconsolable, and nothing I did helped. As I said, this seemed an odd behavior for Mouse because up to that point, he had showed absolutely no interest in the mare whatsoever. Yet at the end of the day, when we tied the two together at the trailer to untack them, he once again stood quietly by Dancer's side as if nothing in the world was ever wrong.

I talk to folks all the time about how it is usually much easier to help a horse through a troubled spot right when it shows up rather than waiting to see if it gets better on its own, or trying to deal with it after it has escalated into something almost unmanageable. For me, this was one of those situations. I certainly don't have any problem with the horses we travel with liking one another or even calling to one another from time to time to check in or find out where the other is. But when the calling or "checking in" starts turning into a disruptive obsession, that's when problems can develop.

So that night, rather than putting Mouse and Dancer back in the same pen together as had been the routine throughout the trip, I asked the clinic host if I could put Mouse in the round pen instead. The round pen was very near the outdoor arena and out of sight of the pen Dancer would be in. So after putting Mouse's hay and water in the pen, he and Dancer went their separate ways for the evening. Even before we reached the round pen gate, Mouse was already looking back and calling for Dancer. Dancer, on the other hand, seemed completely unimpressed and began quietly munching on her hay as soon as she was put in her pen.

About an hour later, there came a knock on the door of my trailer. It was one of the auditors from the clinic, an older woman named Nancy, who was still wearing her nametag from earlier in the day. "I don't know if you knew it or not." She had a concerned smile on her face. "But your gelding is running around and calling pretty loudly over there."

"I know." I smiled reassuringly. "Is he bothering you?"

"Well," she looked toward the pen, then back at me. "No . . . but he seems very upset."

"Oh, I think he's all right." I nodded, stepping out of the trailer and looking toward the round pen, which could just barely be seen through the trees that separated it from where the trailer was parked. "He'll quiet down before long."

"I'll be happy to put him away for you, if you'd like," the woman said, as if not hearing what I had just said.

"He's fine." I smiled. "Really."

"He just seems so upset."

"Yes, he does," I acknowledged. "But he'll feel better soon. I promise."

With that, the woman smiled, nodded, and walked into the barn. Not more than an hour later, there came another knock on my trailer door. This time it was the same woman with two of her friends.

"Evening," I said as I opened the door.

All three women smiled at the same time. "We didn't know if you knew it or not," the older woman said. "But your horse is still running around and calling over there."

"Yes, ma'am. I did know."

"Aren't you going to bring him in?"

"No, ma'am," I said. "Not tonight."

"But he's calling and running!"

"I know. He'll be fine."

"But he seems so upset!" She glanced at her friends, as if looking for one of them to say something.

"He'll feel better before long."

The three women stood looking at me with disapproval, as if I were a youngster who had stolen the apple pie that they left to cool on the windowsill. "Well, I wouldn't leave *my* horse in a pen like that if she were that upset."

"Yes, ma'am."

The three turned and walked back to the barn, and that was the last I saw of them until morning when I went to lead Mouse out of the round pen so I could get him tacked up for the day. All three women were standing near the pen, watching the gelding as he quietly munched on what remained of his hay pile.

"Mornin'," I said as I took Mouse's halter off the fence and opened the gate to the pen. Mouse raised his head as I went in then turned and walked over to me, just as he had every other day for the past few months. I slipped the halter over his nose and led him quietly from the pen.

"He seems better today," the older woman said, almost as if she were upset that he was.

"Yes, ma'am." I nodded. And with that, Mouse was back to his old self. There was no more calling for Dancer throughout the day, and that night, he and Dancer went back in the same pen together. Him being so upset the day before was the one and only occasion during the entire time I owned Mouse that I saw that kind of behavior from him. He hadn't done anything like it before, and didn't do it after.

For whatever reason, on that particular day, he had slipped into an unbalanced state when he wasn't around Dancer. All it took for him to get back in balance was to give him a little time to work it out for himself, which he did. Had the process been interrupted by putting him back in with Dancer before he had a chance to get it worked out, the next time he felt unbalanced without her, his behavior more than likely would have not only escalated but could have also taken longer for him to work through.

As I mentioned before, it can be very difficult for folks to watch a horse as it tries to get itself back into balance after something like this happens. As a result, they will often interrupt the process by "rescuing" the troubled horse and taking it back to its buddy while still in an unbalanced state of mind, thus rewarding that state of mind and inadvertently perpetuating the unbalanced state. So in our attempt to make *ourselves* feel better by not having to watch or listen to the horse go through its natural process of rebalancing, we actually put—and then keep—the horse in an even more unnatural state.

———

Again, it is my belief that all animals, including horses, understand the balance of nature's harmony and how they fit into it. They understand that harmony and confrontation go hand in hand. But rather than making a judgment about it, they simply go about the business of doing what it takes to fit the situation.

A friend of mine who for years had volunteered to help out at the annual *roundup* of the Chincoteague ponies, talks of how the ponies from the various bands on the island were gathered and put into one single large holding pen together. The horses, disoriented and split up from their respective bands in the process, went into a state of disarray, and for a time there was a lot of fighting, squealing, chasing, kicking, and biting. He describes it as looking like a pot of water getting ready to boil over. Yet within about an hour, members of the various bands began to find one another, and as if someone slowly turned down the burner under that boiling pot of water, the activity in the pen died down, and soon all the various bands were back together, grazing separately on the round bales of hay placed around the pen.

Between all the separate bands developed a twenty-foot "no man's land" alley where only the baby horses were allowed to enter and all others were promptly chased back to their band if they entered. A person, however, could easily walk down this twenty-foot alley the horses had developed between themselves without panicking the horses or causing them to go stampeding off.

So in a case like that, not only was each individual horse able to find its own balance even during a most difficult situation, but then that balance began to ripple through each band and eventually through the entire herd. The herd became so balanced that even the introduction of humans into the mix wasn't enough to send the herd back into panic or disarray.

To me, this is a perfect example of nature's harmony the way it is perfectly designed to work. Out of total chaos comes balance. This is not a manufactured balance that is so often searched for and mechanically implemented within the various disciplines of organized horsemanship, but the true balance of nature the way nature designed it. So often these days we get so focused on the "harmony" part of horsemanship that we simply don't allow for, or even allow, the confrontation part of it to show itself.

As a result, our horses, which seem perfectly well adjusted and balanced in the pasture, somehow seem completely unbalanced and unhappy when we are around them. I believe the reason for this isn't that our horses don't like us or don't want to be around us, but rather that they simply aren't allowed to be in balance when they are. I'm not just talking about the physical balance that most folks put so much emphasis on while riding, although that is important too. But rather I'm talking about the horse's emotional balance.

To me, this balance begins and ends with breathing. In fact, breathing is so important to life's overall balance that animals (humans included) can go weeks without food and still stay alive. We can go days without water and still stay alive. But any more than a few short minutes without breathing and we die. Just the act of breathing erratically throughout the day can not only throw off emotional balance, but it can also hinder posture, digestion, reflexes, and blood flow to extremities, among other things.

I can't even begin to count the number of horses (and riders) we see in clinics that come in on the first day of a clinic holding their breath or breathing so erratically that they can't even think. When this occurs in the rider, the person usually can't talk or form thoughts very well, their bodies and hands shake, and they often can't remember what it is that they even want to do with their horse. A nonbreathing horse often can't stand still; they call endlessly and have a tremendous amount of trouble trying to focus or stay focused for long. These issues are not seen much in horses in the wild due to the fact that wild horses (as well as other nondomestic animals) are very good at regulating their breathing so that they stay in balance throughout their day. Even if they do get out of balance due to an attack or trauma of some kind, their bodies will automatically reset back to a normal state, which begins with breathing properly.

Because we humans don't often like to watch, ride, or be around what our horses need to do in order to reset themselves after something has frightened them (for instance), we sometimes find ways to inadvertently stop them from doing what they need to do to reset themselves back to a normal, balanced state. As a result, we often end up teaching them to hold their breath and stay in a perpetual unbalanced state whenever they are around us.

This unbalanced behavior often shows up in an otherwise seasoned and/or well-trained horse by them acting timid or resistant or having trouble transitioning or maintaining speed within a gait. Sometimes they won't be able to maintain a gait at all and they might constantly fall out of a canter or a trot for what seems like no apparent reason. They may also become frightened and suddenly bolt uncontrollably, as in the case of a horse we ran into some time back in one of our clinics.

A very talented and knowledgeable woman named Amy that we had seen and worked with off and on for many years had started this particular horse. She had gotten the gelding under saddle with very little trouble and had spent quite a bit of time riding him both in the arena and on the trail, primarily in the walk and trot, although she had also done a little loping as well.

The horse's owner was relatively new to horses and hadn't done a lot of riding, but the gelding was so quiet that at some point, the owner decided to take him on a short trail ride. To make a long story short, something happened that scared the young horse out on the trail; he spooked, the rider fell off, and the gelding ran back to the barn.

From that point forward this gelding, who up until then had been very quiet, willing, and easy to ride, became spooky, worried, and unpredictable, and often bolted uncontrollably while being ridden. The horse was sent back to Amy to see if she could get the problem resolved, and while things had gotten a little better under her care, the bolting and spookiness remained.

To see if they could get to the root of the problem, the horse was brought to a clinic we were doing nearby, and in bringing the gelding to the round pen, it was clear he was not feeling good inside. Just bringing him one hundred yards from the barn to the round pen, the gelding spooked three or four times and called loudly to no one in particular. Once inside the round pen, he took off running but then scared himself when he saw his own reflection in the side of a black trailer that was parked next to the pen, and stopped.

After watching the gelding for a short time, it became clear that he wasn't breathing very well at all. For whatever reason, he was going through the same thing a lot of domestic horses do. After being frightened as badly as he had been, his body didn't get a chance to naturally reset back to normal, and as a result, he was staying in a perpetual state of heightened awareness.

In this case, the solution was simple. We just needed to get the young horse breathing again. Amy had volunteered to work with him during the clinic. I asked her to put him on a longe line and then canter him in the pen until he began breathing properly. In the canter, when a horse is breathing properly, they will exhale every time they push off on their outside hind foot. So when in the right lead, they would breathe out on the left hind, and on the left lead, right hind.

Now, when I say this solution was simple, it was. But for this horse, it wasn't easy. What had happened with this gelding after the initial incident on the trail was he had been inadvertently *trained* to hold his breath whenever he was around people. The accident on the trail frightened and traumatized him, which, for whatever reason, he hadn't been able to get resolved in his mind or body at the time. He was then caught and put away while still holding his breath and in a state of worry or perhaps even near panic.

All animals associate the way they feel with the last thing they saw or experienced when they became traumatized. So because it was a human the gelding had the accident with and then a human that put him away while he was still scared, he naturally associated humans with not only becoming frightened in the first place, but he also associated them with him feeling bad. So, from that point forward, every time he had dealings with humans, he automatically went into a heightened state of nervousness and worry, which always began with him holding his breath.

By the time he had been brought to the clinic, he was spooking at everything and trying to bolt and/or run off anytime he became even a little scared while being ridden. Of course, him bolting was nature's way of beginning the process of resetting his mind and body back to a normal state. However, the people working with him saw it (and understandably so) as a potentially dangerous behavior and would shut him down any time he tried to run, thus inadvertently stopping him from resetting himself. So, over time, the gelding had simply been trained to maintain a frantic and unbalanced state of mind whenever people were around or were handling him.

On that first day of the clinic, the gelding cantered nonstop around the inside of the round pen for over twenty minutes in one direction before he finally started breathing properly—an indicator of how stuck he was emotionally. Most horses that aren't breathing around people due to being involved with some kind of traumatic situation will usually begin breathing within ten to twenty laps. This horse zipped passed twenty laps in the first three minutes.

Once he was breathing properly in the first direction, we reversed him and went the other way, which took an additional ten minutes before he was breathing properly. Altogether, this horse ran nearly nonstop for thirty minutes before his mind and body finally went into the process of resetting itself. By the next day, his spooking and seemingly mindless calling had disappeared, and by the third day Amy was up and riding him, with him showing absolutely no signs of being the troubled horse we saw on the first day.

I was able to talk with Amy a year later and found that not only was the horse doing really well, but the owner was also riding and working with him on a regular basis, and they were both getting along great together.

In this case the catalyst for such a change came less from any training that may have occurred, although that was certainly important, and more from the fact that the horse was able to regain his emotional and physical balance by doing nothing more than allowing humans to help him engage the "reset" system nature had already provided him with.

———————

As I mentioned earlier, it has been my work in aikido, as well as my work with horses, that has brought me to the understanding that this synchronization that we call harmony isn't a fixed location we end up in and never leave, but rather a point that continuously comes and goes like the changing of the seasons. At times it might stay with us for longer periods than others, but eventually something—a thought, a word, an action—will no doubt cause it to slip away. Even then, however, nature has supplied us with all of the tools we need to get back into balance once we have lost our way, and whether in our work with horses or in our work with each other, all we need to do is try to understand and look for its development rather than try and hold on to it once we've achieved it.

Chapter 3
Spirit of the Horse

_____

I've had a cell phone for a long time. But unlike a lot of folks who own them, I almost never have mine with me. It either stays in the console of the truck when I'm traveling or on the kitchen counter when I'm home, but seldom, if ever, do I actually have it on me. On this day, both it and I were in the house when it rang. It was on the kitchen counter, and I was looking out the front window at the spring snowstorm that was just getting underway. "Hello?" I said as I flipped the little phone open and put it to my ear.

"They're going to take him!" It was my good friend Tim, and I immediately knew what, and who, he was talking about.

"That's great, Tim!" I said. "When?"

"End of the month" was his enthusiastic reply. "After all this time, and everything we've been through, he finally gets to go back where he belongs."

"That's really great," I repeated.

Tim and I had met several years earlier when he sponsored a clinic for me at his farm in Rhode Island. At the time he had known me only from my books, and while he was excited to host the clinic and enthusiastically booked the riders' spots, he would later tell me that the main reason he wanted me to come to his place was so he could get help with his six-year-old mustang, Tico.

The day after we arrived at his place in Rhode Island, Tim took my assistant and I out to breakfast and gave us the particulars of who would be riding in the clinic and when they would be riding. Toward the end of breakfast, almost, it seemed, as an afterthought, he asked if I did any colt starting in my clinics. I explained that I used to start colts in my clinics but found that the kind of colt starting that I did and the kind of colt starting most people were looking for in a clinic situation didn't really suit one another, so I had stopped the practice several years earlier.

I told him that the majority of the people I had run into over the years were looking for a much quicker start on their young horses than I was comfortable helping them with. After trying several different ways of presenting colt starting in clinics, and not finding anything I was happy with, I finally decided to abandon the whole idea.

I had heard this question before from other new clinic hosts, and normally after my explanation, the subject is dropped, even though I always got the feeling either the host had a colt they wanted help with, or they knew someone else who did. Tim, on the other hand, was undaunted by my explanation and, if anything, seemed relieved by what I had said. Not relieved about me saying I didn't do colt starting but rather relieved that I thought too many people wanted their colts started too fast.

"I've got a horse back at the farm that I'm looking to get started under saddle," he said. "He's a six-year-old mustang that I've been using as a stallion . . . a really nice horse but hasn't had a lot of handling." He looked like he was going to pause for a second, but then didn't. "He's just a real special horse, and I don't want to do anything to ruin him."

"Well," I said, gently sliding my now empty plate off to the side of the table so it would be easier for the waitress to retrieve. "Like I said, I don't really do colt starting anymore."

"I completely understand," he said. "And I totally agree with you. Colts are started way too fast in clinics these days." This time, he did pause. "I guess I'm not really looking for someone to help me get him started as much as someone who can give me a direction to go with him. He's not like any horse I've ever had before, and besides, I don't really care how long it takes to get him under saddle."

I had heard people refer to their horses as "special" in the past, and what I have come to find is that the horse is special to them, but not necessarily what I or someone else might refer to as a "special" horse. I had also had people tell me that they didn't care how long it took to get their young horse under saddle before, only to find out that what they really meant was that they don't care how long it takes, as long as it's relatively quick.

"Maybe you could take a look at him when we get back to the farm and see what you think," Tim suggested. "If he doesn't seem like something you want to work with in the clinic, I understand."

"Sounds good."

Later that morning, after Tim cordially gave us a tour of the island his place was on, we headed back to the farm. Once there, he had to see to a couple things, and I wanted to check on our horses that we had put out on pasture earlier that morning. Before we split up, Tim gave me directions to his horse's pen, and we agreed to meet there thirty minutes later.

After checking on our horses, who were obviously very happy to be out of the trailer and able to stretch their legs for the first time in three days, I made my way over to where

43

Tim said his horse's pen was. It may be noteworthy here to mention that I have had the opportunity to work with quite a few mustangs over the years. For the most part, they all looked relatively the same, usually sort of rangy with many, certainly not all, of them bay in color, with long manes and tails, good bones and feet, and they often had a mild to pronounced roman nose. Many of them usually had similar movement as well, efficient and powerful. I had no reason to think I would see anything other than an average mustang as I rounded the corner of the building to the pen where Tim's horse was being kept.

What I was greeted with as I came around the barn and over to the pen, however, was anything but an average, run-of-the-mill mustang. While this horse had many of the physical characteristics of other wild horses I had seen or worked with over the years, what I wasn't expecting was this horse's almost overwhelming presence of *spirit*.

Now, over time the word *spirit,* when used in relationship to horses, has taken on a sort of convoluted connotation. For me, the word has always referred to the pure *essence* of the horse. That inner part of the animal they are all born with and, which left untouched or unaltered by man, allows the horse the power to not only stay true to who they are as an individual, but it also provides them the power to be an essential and vital member of the entire herd. It is the part of the horse that has been carefully crafted by millions of years of evolution to ensure the survival of both the individual and the species as a whole. This was the element of the horse that trainers of old wanted to alter or "break" in order to get the horse to become usable for either work or transportation or both—and is also the part of the horse that, in my opinion, has been intentionally watered down by humans through centuries of selective breeding of the domestic horse.

These days, with the vast majority of horses having not had the luxury of being born into a life without man's intervention, it could be argued that most, if not all, domestic horses now possess a lack of what one might refer to as that "ancient spirit," the part of the horse that has been completely untouched by man and which makes a horse a horse.

As a result, most horse people may have never experienced or even seen that ancient horse *spirit*, and because of that, erratic, high-strung, or even simply animated behavior, which has either inadvertently or even purposely been trained or bred into the horse, ends up being mistaken for the horse's *spirit*. In other words, the word *spirit* no longer refers to the horse's internal and external *presence* as dictated by nature, but rather it usually just refers to a horse's *man-made* behavior.

This horse of Tim's, on the other hand, was different. I could almost feel this horse's presence even before I could see him, and I think Tim knew it because as I neared the pen, he turned with a smile and said, "See what I mean about him being special?"

The horse, who Tim had named Atlantico or Tico for short, was standing alone in a pen that measured around forty feet by sixty feet. He was alert, but not frightened, and at just over 14.2 hands, he was about average height for a mustang. He was heavier boned and thicker muscled than most of the mustangs I'd seen, however, with a broader forehead and more refined face and was almost completely void of the roman nose I was accustomed to seeing in the typical wild horse. A small white star on his forehead was his only marking, and as I got near the gate where Tim was standing, the horse let out a warning snort.

"Wow," was all I could say as I stood looking at him.

"He's out of the Sulphur herd," Tim said. "From out near Sulphur Springs, Utah. I got him when he was eighteen months old, used him as a breeding stallion up until about a year ago, and just had him gelded a few months back. I really haven't handled him much, but would sure like to start working with him."

The gelding let out another snort then whirled over his hindquarters and trotted off to the back of the pen, where he whirled back and let out another snort.

"I'm not in any hurry with him at all," Tim added. "Getting him under saddle would be my ultimate goal, but I really don't care how long that takes." He turned toward the gelding. "I feel that this horse has a really strong spirit." He looked back at me. "My main concern is that whatever happens during his training, that his spirit stay intact, and if I can't get him under saddle without that happening, then I don't want to do it." Tico snorted again. "Do you think that's possible?"

It was a question nobody had ever asked me before. I had had plenty of people over the years ask me how long I thought the training of their horse was going to take, but never anyone that expressed concern about keeping the horse's spirit intact while it was happening.

As I watched Tico move cautiously around his pen, my first thought was that anyone who was that concerned about the horse's well-being probably wouldn't ruin its spirit to begin with, even unintentionally. And my second thought was that I was pretty sure this particular horse wasn't going to allow someone to take that spirit from him anyway, not without a fight and not without someone getting hurt. Either way, Tico was going to be fine.

"Yes," I said, turning back to Tim. "I think it's possible."

———————

My first opportunity to work with Tico was the next day during the clinic. We spent all of our time primarily teaching him to allow Tim to approach and catch him, something that had been extremely difficult for him in the past. Now, at the risk of anthropomorphizing, almost as soon as I walked into Tico's pen I started to get the feeling that he thought some kind of terrible mistake had been made. After all, it was one thing to have been taken from his home range and then placed in a pasture with other horses, having only occasional and minimal contact with humans. But now, not only had he been taken from the pasture and his pasture mates and placed in this pen by himself, it also appeared that humans were suddenly way more interested in him than they had ever been before, or that he was comfortable with.

His whole world up until then had revolved solely around either survival in the wild or the camaraderie of other horses while in captivity. The concept of him being asked to allow humans to get close appeared so foreign to him that it must have seemed like he'd landed on another planet. In his world, there were only horses and horse behavior. Human contact was not something he needed, or wanted, and it appeared as though he simply couldn't understand why we were so intent on getting him to change his mind.

I remember working with him on that first day and thinking (again, at the risk of sounding anthropomorphic) that he must have felt like someone who had been charged and convicted of a crime he didn't commit, then unceremoniously thrown in prison for it. Just like an innocent prisoner, Tico seemed to spend most of his time during those first days of handling not only vigorously proclaiming his innocence but also trying in every way he could to tell us that he didn't belong with humans. Still, over the next few days of very quiet and consistent work, and I think through sheer repetition more than anything else, Tico grudgingly learned to allow humans to approach, touch, and even catch him.

I think sometimes we humans automatically assume that animals, even wild ones, should just somehow *want* to be with us. As if some innate desire suddenly washes over them whenever humans are present, and just like that, they become domesticated. I guess in a humanly perfect world, that would sure be nice. However, that way of thinking doesn't take into account the fact that animals like Tico, who are not only born into a world without humans but also come from a long line of "humanless" ancestors, had long ago developed a void where people are concerned. They don't need, nor have they ever needed, humans for their own survival, and so they don't really even know how to look to us for help, nor do they seem to even want to.

There was recently a study done that bore this out. In the study, a litter of domestic dog puppies and a litter of wolf pups both born to parents being kept in captivity were raised exactly the same way by exactly the same researchers over exactly the same period of time. Both the domestic pups and the wolf pups became friendly and compliant toward the human researchers working with them. However, after both litters of pups were old enough, the researches set up a series of experiments. In one very telling experiment, a one foot by one inch box built of heavy wire was set up and a piece of meat attached to a leather strap was placed in the middle of the box. All the pups had to do to get the meat was pull on the strap which protruded from the box and the piece of meat would slide out from underneath. The pups from both litters did very well learning this particular task.

Then the researchers set up the exact same experiment with one difference. The strap that the meat was attached to was now also attached to the bottom of the box, so it became impossible for the meat to be removed. Immediately, the difference between the domestic pups and the wolf pups became apparent. After three or four tries at retrieving the immovable leather strap, the domestic pups stopped trying and went straight to the researchers. Each one sat down next to the human and began looking back and forth between the researcher's face and the leather strap.

The wolf pups, on the other hand, did something different. Even when it became clear that the strap wouldn't budge, they continued pulling at it. They also tried to dig under the box, pry the box open, bite and pull at the wire, and when all else failed, they simply stopped all attempts and lay down near the box. Looking to the humans for help retrieving the meat didn't even seem to enter their minds.

What the researchers were seeing was the pups' inherent wolf behavior still intact, even though those particular wolf pups had been born into captivity. In other words, the essence of the wolf, that part of the wolf that can easily survive on its own without having to rely on the overt help of another species, was still very prevalent in the individual animal. It was that same essence that I feel is built into all wild creatures that I believed we were seeing in Tico's behavior whenever we worked with him. It showed up not only during that particular clinic in Rhode Island but also in all the subsequent times in which Tim and I worked with him.

In keeping with Tim's commitment to not do anything during Tico's training that would harm Tico's spirit, the work during the next two years had gone painfully slowly. By the middle of the second year, however, Tim had not only quietly and successfully been able to saddle and mount Tico, but he was even beginning to take him on short rides around the property. By the third year, Tim and Tico were doing some pretty extensive trail riding, and they had even participated in the local Fourth of July parade—another goal Tim had hoped to achieve with Tico.

All outward signs pointed toward Tico seemingly beginning to settle into his new life as a domesticated horse and willing partner for Tim. Still, I could never really shake the feeling that Tico, while certainly making good progress under Tim's quiet and patient tutelage, was still that "innocent prisoner" trying to get someone to listen to him as he pleaded his case for his release.

The signs were very subtle, but they were always there. Even after over three years of consistent handling, Tico was still a little erratic when it came to allowing himself to be caught. He would also scoot around nervously from time to time when Tim would get on him. He would sometimes get wide-eyed and defensive around other horses on the trails and he was still very wary of humans in general, especially anybody whom he hadn't met before.

In and of themselves, none of these issues are really anything to be overly concerned about, especially for a horse that spent the first six years of his life being feral. Still, I found Tico's propensity for not wanting to be caught concerning. It wasn't that he didn't like being caught that was troublesome, but rather it was the way he looked when he did it. After three years, Tico didn't look any different in the way his body moved or in the way he acted when he didn't want to be caught than he did on the very first day we worked with him on it.

That bothered me because it seemed that whatever he was trying to say to us on that very first day, and what he was still saying three years later, hadn't changed at all. In other words, while he may have been doing the things he had been trained to do, his overall opinion of the situation hadn't seemed to change much, nor was he letting go of it. Just like that innocent prisoner who, over time, finds a way to get along while in prison, but also never loses sight of the fact that he never committed the crime for which he was being detained in the first place. It's the spirit that keeps reminding the man that while prison may be where he lives, being there will never make him a criminal.

That was the feeling I got whenever I watched Tico moving away from Tim during those times when he didn't want to be caught. He may have been in a pen, but it didn't make him a domestic horse.

———————

I didn't hear about the wreck from Tim, but rather a mutual friend who was visiting Colorado at the time. "Did you hear what happened to Tim?" she had asked, almost as an afterthought one afternoon.

"No."

"I guess he and Tico had a pretty bad accident." She continued, "Tim broke some ribs, cut his face up real bad, and ended up with a concussion."

"I hadn't heard," I said, trying to hide my concern. "When?"

"A month and a half ago, or so."

"What happened?"

She explained that Tim and his fianceé Trudy, along with a neighbor, had been out riding for several hours and were on their way back home when they decided to take a shortcut. The path they chose was steep and covered in rocks, branches, and other debris, which was nothing new for any of them or their horses. As they started down the hill, Tico stepped on a branch buried under some tall grass. The branch swung up and hit Tico right between his hind legs, which scared him and caused him to buck . . . hard. Tim came off, got his foot hung up in the stirrup, and had gotten dragged.

"Tico bucked?" I asked, making sure I had heard her correctly.

"I guess so," she said. "That's what I heard, anyway."

"That's not good." I thought I only said the words in my head, but apparently, they came out of my mouth too.

"What's not good?" my friend asked. "The fact that Tim got hurt or that Tico bucked?"

"Both."

Of course I was concerned about Tim's health, and later that evening, I called him to find out how he was doing and to hear what happened straight from him. But of equal concern to me was the fact that not only had Tico bucked, but that Tim had come off while he was doing it. I had mentioned to Tim early on in Tico's training that I felt Tico wasn't a bucker, and if something scared him or if he was uncomfortable with something that was going on when someone was on his back, he would more than likely choose to flee from it rather than buck. Up until the day of the accident, that was exactly what Tico had done anytime he was frightened by something. He scooted or tried to run from it, but he had never tried to buck.

Bucking hadn't been an option for Tico up till then because he had never tried it. Now, however, not only had he tried it, but he had also successfully dislodged Tim from his back by doing it. It was disconcerting because I was afraid that Tico would not only start seeing bucking as a viable option in stressful situations, but that he might also turn to it with more frequency in the future.

Just a few weeks later, I received a call from Tim in which he told me he and Tico had been on a ride and a branch brushed against Tico's hind legs, which caused him to buck again. And again, Tim had come off. This time, however, Tim was able to get back on and finish the ride, but I could tell from the tone in Tim's voice that this time the damage had been done. I felt just from listening to him on the phone that Tim's once unshakable trust in Tico had developed a sizable hole in it and, from the way he was talking, I wasn't sure it was ever going to be repaired.

Undaunted, Tim continued to work with Tico, making every effort to find ways to help him feel better about things touching him (something that, before the first accident, hadn't been a problem), and he'd still been riding him, although not as much as he had been.

A few months later, Tim and Trudy, along with my wife Crissi and I, all met up in Florida for a few days of rest before Crissi and I had to start a series of winter clinics throughout the south. We had all camped and ridden in the same area in the past, and Tim and Tico had always done really well out on the trails there. But on this trip, things were markedly different between the two. Tico was much more adamant about not being caught, and he was continuously on edge even after he was. Under saddle, he was perpetually tense and anxious and never really found a way to quiet himself.

Tim appeared to be struggling as well. An experienced and normally bold and confident rider, Tim now seemed uncharacteristically cautious and wary. While on the one and only trail ride we were able to take during our time there, Tim spent almost as much time leading Tico as he did riding him, and even when he did ride, he wasn't the same calmly assertive person I was accustomed to seeing in the past. As I watched the two of them interact out on the trail, I couldn't help but think that if they weren't at end of the relationship Tim had worked so hard to try and develop with Tico, they weren't far from it.

While out on the trail Tico spooked and scooted a number of times over shadows on the trail, noises in the woods, and wind rustling through the trees. Tim handled each one of Tico's spooks well but would follow almost each one by asking me if I thought he could have done something different or better to help Tico through it.

The truth of the matter was, I'm not sure there was anything Tim could have done differently or better. In fact, in the big scheme of things, I really don't know of anybody that could have done a better job with Tico's overall training than Tim had. At this point, I didn't believe training was the issue. The issue was that Tico had gone as far as he could go, both figuratively and literally. He simply wasn't a domestic saddle horse, never had been and never would be.

A horse like Tico didn't have it in him to turn his decision making over to someone else, no matter how much we humans hoped he could. He was a wild horse, plain and simple, and hard wired that way right out of the box. To his immense credit, he had done everything that had been asked of him to the very best of his ability, but it was becoming clear that in order for him to remain true to himself, even that was going to have to come to an end. Tico, it seemed, was actually beginning to revert to his wild state.

"To be honest, Tim," I said as we rode along the sandy trail. "I think he's given you all he has to give. This may be a good time to give some thought to whether or not you want to keep riding him."

"I think you may be right," Tim replied, a hint of sadness in his voice.

After Crissi and I left Florida for Georgia, and then went on to Arizona after that, Tim and Trudy remained at the little campground in Florida to do some more riding. A month and a half had passed when I received another call from Tim. He and Tico had had another wreck. They had been riding out on the trails when an obviously agitated Tico suddenly bolted into the woods and went bucking. Apparently, Tim had stayed with him until it became clear one or both of them were going to get hurt, or worse if he didn't get off, so Tim had picked the best spot he could find and did just that.

Tim landed hard on a fallen log and broke another rib. While still on the ground, Trudy told him in no uncertain terms that she did not want Tim to ever get on Tico's back again. It wasn't a hard sell. Tim had already made the same decision himself. As for Tico, he never looked back but rather ran for all he was worth the two miles back through the woods and all the way to the trailhead. There, a neighbor caught him and put him in a round pen until Tim could come and retrieve him.

During their time together, Tim and Tico had been through a lot. From the first days of working on catching Tico back in Rhode Island, to a number of clinics in Florida and

New Hampshire, to hundreds of miles of trails and even a Fourth of July parade. Through it all, Tim had remained true to his promise to keep Tico's spirit intact no matter what. And it was now that same spirit that Tim was going to continue to protect.

"Every day," Tim said during our phone conversation, "I'm watching his spirit fade." There was a pause. "He's not happy, and neither am I."

"Then it's time to make a change," I said, supporting his decision.

We began discussing options for Tico's future. Tim wondered if I wanted him or if I knew of someone who did. I told him I didn't. I didn't come right out and say it at the time, but as far as I was concerned Tico was a horse that should have never been taken out of the wild to begin with, and keeping him in captivity any longer than was necessary just wasn't the right thing to do.

During our talk, we discussed several options for Tico, all of them viable, but none terribly practical, and then I remembered hearing about a wild horse sanctuary somewhere up in the Dakotas. "I think it's in the Black Hills," I told Tim. "I've heard a lot of really good things about them. Maybe they'd be worth trying to get a hold of."

Over the next couple days, Tim was able to contact the folks at the Black Hills Wild Horse Sanctuary in Hot Springs, South Dakota, and discuss the possibility of Tico going there to live. Apparently, Tico's story wasn't an unfamiliar one to them, and while sympathetic to Tim and Tico's situation, the sanctuary was right on the verge of having their maximum number of horses for the number of acres they had. Before they could commit to taking Tico, they would need to discuss it with the powers that be, and they would get back with Tim as soon as they could.

Nearly a month had passed before I received the next phone call from Tim. "They're going to take him!" It had been a long time since I'd heard Tim that enthusiastic when he talked about Tico.

"When?" I had asked.

"The end of the month," Tim replied.

"That's great."

"Yeah," Tim agreed. Then after a short pause he added, "I'll be sad to see him go ... but happy that he'll finally be in a place where he really belongs."

"Me too."

———————

Just like that innocent prisoner who never loses sight of the fact that he isn't a criminal, Tico never lost sight of the fact that he wasn't a domestic horse. To Tico's credit, he held on to who and what he was with everything he had. And to Tim's credit, he never did anything to Tico that took that away from him. It's a difficult thing for a human being to own a horse whose spirit is so strong and yet be selfless enough to not want to alter it in some way—to leave the essence of the horse still in the horse. And yet that is exactly what Tim had done. Right up till the end, Tim allowed Tico's nature to shine through, and when he realized Tico could no longer live in a human's world without causing damage to who Tico was, Tim set him free.

Seldom do we get a chance in life to see two individuals who are so well connected to each other that they will do whatever the other needs, even though it may be extremely difficult for both. Tim did everything he could to leave Tico's spirit in tact, and in return, Tico became a domesticated horse for Tim, right up until he couldn't anymore.

When Tico began to revert to his wild state, Tim found a place for him to go where he could once again thrive. It was a perfect balance, an example of nature's give and take between two individuals of different species—each one looking out for the best interest of the other, and then both realizing, and also respecting, the fact that their time together had come to an end.

I believe that sometimes the mark of a true horseman isn't just about what a person can do with a horse; it's also what they don't do with them. That, too, can be a very delicate balance, the kind we are surrounded with in nature, and the type of thing we don't really see much anymore in horse/human relationships.

As Tim had promised in the very beginning, Tico's spirit did, indeed, remain unaltered. But in the end, it had also been Tim's spirit, and the true horseman in him, that allowed that to come to pass.

Chapter 4
Self-Protection

We were waiting for the next horse and rider to come into the arena at a clinic in California when one of the auditors raised her hand.

"Yes, ma'am?" I said.

"I'd be interested in hearing what you do when a horse bites you."

I had to give the question some thought. It had been quite a long time since I'd been bit. In fact it had been so long that I couldn't really even remember the last time it happened.

"I mean," she continued, "what's the best way to protect yourself when that happens?"

"Well," I started. "The best way to protect yourself is to not get bit in the first place—"

"I mean," she interrupted, "there are trainers who say that once a horse bites you, you have three seconds to beat the snot out of them. But after that, you have to leave them alone. Is that what you do?"

"First of all," I said, "if you're hitting the horse *after* he's bitten you, that isn't self-defense, it's retaliation. Those are two different things. Second, I would want to know why the horse is biting in the first place before I tried to stop them from doing it. Without knowing the cause, it would be hard to fix the issue no matter what you do to or with the horse."

"So you don't subscribe to the 'three-second rule'?" she questioned. "The reason I ask is that I have a horse at home that bites, and I've been using it on him."

"Has it been working?"

"Not really." She chuckled. "Now he bites me and then backs away before I can hit him back."

"I see."

This woman's question wasn't an uncommon one. People ask similar questions all the time. *What should I do when my horse bites me, what should I do when my horse kicks me, what should I do when my horse bucks me off or strikes at me or runs me over.* When one listens carefully to these questions, it's easy to pick out the common thread in all them. The person isn't asking how to prevent the unwanted behavior from happening; they are asking what to do *after* it already has. I have always found this type of question interesting because the person asking it is looking at a situation that might happen in the future, but doing so from a past tense perspective—"*This might happen, so after it does, what should I do?*"

Basically, these folks have already put themselves in the role of a victim. It's like asking what one should do if they are walking down the street and an ominous-looking person walks up, pulls a gun, and shoots them in the leg. It seems to me the options for self-protection at that point are relatively limited. On the other hand, if a person asks what to do if they get a bad feeling about someone who is approaching them, that's different. In a case

like that, the person is looking at the situation from a preventive standpoint as opposed to the standpoint of being a target. Because they are looking ahead instead of back, the options for what to do to protect themselves become almost unlimited.

My dad always used to say that it's easier to stay out of trouble than it is to get out of trouble. Perhaps another way to say it is an ounce of prevention is worth a pound of cure. Either way, getting out ahead of a problem is always better than trying to fix it once in the middle of it. So when we talk about folks finding ways to stay safe while around horses, what we are really doing is talking about the person taking a proactive approach to the situation rather than a sit-back-and-see-what-happens kind of approach.

Self-protection is an extremely important part of nature . . . perhaps *the* most important part. Without it, very few species of animals on the planet would be here today. In fact, pretty much anytime a horse acts up or acts out, self protection is usually the primary cause. Unlike a lot of people, horses don't sit back and wait to see if something or someone is going to harm them. When they feel a threat of any kind, they take immediate and decisive action, and only after they feel there is no longer a threat do they stop to see what the problem actually was. Most people, on the other hand, do just the opposite. They sit back to see if there is a problem then do something only after it is apparent that a problem actually exists, and sometimes not even then!

I was once asked if I thought this "sitting back" was due to a lack of focus on the part of the human. My answer was that if anything, in those situations, the human might actually be focusing too much. In other words, the person may be so focused on the fact that their horse, who, for instance, is usually very quiet, calm, and friendly, is suddenly acting out of sorts, that they don't even see the horse (who is perhaps being frightened by a paper bag being blown across the street) getting ready to jump right on top of them, or right out from underneath them.

I know that may sound strange, but situations like this are actually much more common than one might think. We see them all the time. A person gets so focused on their horse's uncharacteristic or unwanted behavior (for example), that they don't even see the kick or the bite or the strike or the buck coming. The next thing they know they're lying on the ground hurt, and they don't really even know how it happened! Yet, they were so completely focused on the symptom—the horse's uncharacteristic behavior—that they didn't see the cause, and they certainly didn't see the end result even as it was heading their way. This ability to be "hyper focused," if you will, is nothing out of the ordinary, and in fact, it actually has a name. The scientific term for this degree of focus is *inattentional blindness*, and it is hardwired into the human brain.

Here's a very telling example of inattentional blindness. Several years ago, NASA did an experiment with a large number of commercial airline pilots. In this experiment, the pilots, while in a simulator, were to do a series of routine landings. Each pilot landed his or her aircraft on the runway numerous times without any trouble. Then the researchers placed a Boeing 747 on the runway right where the pilots were to land, and 75 percent of the pilots landed right on top of the 747. These pilots, all of them very experienced, would later say that they never saw the plane on the runway, even though it was right there in front of them the entire time.

The reason? They were only focused on performing their landing correctly and, as a result, never became aware of the plane on the runway. Because of this, their brain never registered that a plane was even there. In other words, if something is literally directly in front of us but we aren't specifically looking for that one thing, our brain will have a tendency to shut it out and not even bring it in to our consciousness.

Humans, more than any other species, have the ability to get so fixated on certain specific things that we can actually become blind to certain, extremely obvious other things. For instance, the leading cause of head-on car collisions is the fact that when most drivers see a car heading straight for them, they get so fixated on that car heading their way that they drive directly into it instead of looking for a way to escape the collision.

So as we can see, *lack* of focus is seldom the problem when dealing with a potentially dangerous or harmful situation, whether with a horse or anything else in life. What often *is* the problem, however, and the thing that ends up getting most people in trouble, is simply an overall lack of *awareness* often brought on by inattentional blindness, and that is one thing animals don't have to deal with.

Unlike people, the way animals' brains work is they can take in a lot of information all at once and not really have to process any of it. As a result, animals are aware but not necessarily focused on everything in their immediate, and even not so immediate, surroundings. Animals don't necessarily need to know what something is, they basically just need to know whether or not to run from it (in the case of prey animals) or eat it (in the case of predators).

Because of the higher function of a human brain, however, we are designed to process almost everything that we see so we can understand what the thing is. That way, if our ancient ancestors looked at a big brown rock from a distance, and saw and understood it was a big brown rock instead of a buffalo, they wouldn't waste time stalking the rock, thinking it might be something they could kill and eat. They could look at the rock, immediately know it was a rock, and move on. A horse, on the other hand, might look at that same rock, see the shadows it is creating on the ground and in the crevices on its face, and not know what it was. All they would know is that it doesn't look right to them, and they should stay away from it. It's a sort if information bypass, if you will.

On the other end of the spectrum, the human brain is so geared toward understanding that if we see something that we've never seen before or that doesn't make sense to us, our brain will often make up a story for us so that we *can* make sense of it, even though the story may not match up with the reality of the situation.

It is for that reason that most horse people will almost always have some kind of a story behind their horse's unexpected, uncharacteristic, or unwanted behavior. For instance, I once had a woman tell me that her horse was deathly afraid of squirrels. The reason she believed that was the case was because she had been on a trail ride with her horse when a squirrel leapt from a nearby bush and scampered noisily up a tree. When that happened, the horse spooked, spun, and the woman fell off.

The woman's brain associated the squirrel with the horse's uncharacteristic behavior, and so it immediately came to the conclusion that the horse was afraid of squirrels, when in reality, it probably wasn't the squirrel that the horse was afraid of at all, as much as it was the squirrel's sudden and unexpected movement. You see, horses (as well as most other animals) are so aware that they literally see everything in their surroundings. But if something, say a squirrel, is in the bushes and out of the horse's sight, then the squirrel, as far as the horse is concerned, doesn't exist. So if the horse is walking along a trail and something (the squirrel) suddenly appears out of nowhere, making a lot of commotion and then scampers up a tree, that would naturally give the horse a pretty good fright.

As I said, horses don't need to process the fact that the thing making the noise and running up the tree is a squirrel. They only need to know that there is sudden and unexpected movement in very close proximity to where they are, and that is almost never a good thing when you are an animal designed to be another animal's lunch. On the other hand, we humans see the squirrel running up the tree and almost immediately understand it that it is a squirrel, and because we don't see or understand the world the same way a prey animal does, we automatically assume the horse is afraid of squirrels when in reality, the horse probably never even saw the squirrel in the first place, only the movement caused by the squirrel.

Along those same lines, I was talking to a lady once who said she had attended one of those European horse extravaganzas in which horses and riders charge around the arena, jump through hoops of fire, run past exploding cannons, perform intricate patterns at a dead run, dance around on their hind legs, and perform any number of other hair-raising feats, all of which are done in front of several thousand screaming and cheering spectators.

She said that when the show was over, one of the stars rode his horse over to the stands, dismounted, took off the cape he was wearing, and placed it over his horse's saddle.

The horse stood quietly while the performer signed autographs and visited with the people. He stood quietly, that is, right up until the cape that the man had placed over the saddle slipped from the horse's back and fell to the ground. At that point, this seemingly fearless horse that had just been in the middle of all that chaos in the arena, shied away from the cape. The woman then told me how struck she was by the fact that we humans can teach a horse to do almost anything, but even then, no matter how skilled or how highly trained the horse becomes, they are all still just horses on the inside.

What this woman now understands is that just because the horse has been domesticated over thousands of years doesn't mean they are void of their natural makeup. And part of that makeup dictates that regardless of age, breed, or training, a horse's instinctive self-protection system is turned on all the time. As a result, they are always on the lookout for anything out of the ordinary, such as sudden movements or sounds; changes in patterns, colors, or shapes; strange odors; or even strange shadows or variations of light.

By constantly being on guard, there is then no need for them to be able to distinguish between a squirrel running up a tree, a cape falling off a saddle, or a lion jumping out of a bush. To the horse, these things all hold the same importance, at least initially, and so will elicit pretty much the same response. All of this falls under nature's rules of survival, if you will, and is one of the ways she keeps the horse, and the species, alive and vibrant.

Humans, on the other hand, have a tendency to live under slightly different rules of survival. Over the years we have slowly gone from paying very close attention to the laws of nature to paying closer attention to the laws of man. As a rule, we humans no longer need to be terribly vigilant about our surroundings because we have man-made laws to protect us against most potentially dangerous situations we might come up against while living in a world with other humans.

Society now has rules and laws against other people attacking us, trying to kill us, taking our stuff from us or breaking into our homes, all things we had to watch out for back when we all still lived in caves. We have rules for driving our vehicles on the road and even for how we park them on the side of the road. We have rules and laws for the way we hunt and fish, and for that matter, most outdoor areas, particularly government-owned areas, even have laws and rules for what we can and cannot do when we are out in the woods or out hiking on the trails. In fact, pretty much anything we do as a society has some kind of law or limitation placed on it that is designed to keep us safe from each other in one way or another.

So basically what all this boils down to is that while animals, regardless of their level of domestication, still live under the rules of self-protection designed by nature, humans on the other hand, for the most part, have turned the majority of their individual self-protection over to the man-made laws that govern society. In and of itself this isn't necessarily a bad thing, particularly because when everybody plays by the rules, because the rules do exactly what they were designed to do . . . keep everybody safe.

The rules we live under aren't the problem. The problem, I believe, is that we as a society have become relatively complacent when it comes to our own self-protection because it has been so ingrained in us that the laws and rules designed by man will keep us safe from harm. And the truth of the matter is these laws and rules will keep us safe, unless someone decides not to play by the rules. *This* is where most people get in trouble. We automatically assume everybody is playing by the same set of man-made rules that we are, so when someone doesn't play by those rules, we often find ourselves totally unprepared to deal with what's happening, and we end up at the mercy of the person or situation we have just found ourselves in.

There is an old saying in the martial arts world that states, *if someone jumps out of the bushes and attacks you, that's their problem. If you are too frightened to do anything about it, that's your problem.* Because we automatically assume that everybody is playing under the same set of rules, most people have a difficult time dealing with a situation where someone they come in contact with, say a mugger on the street, is breaking those rules. The person being attacked doesn't know what to do, and even if they did know what to do, many times they wouldn't know *how* to do it. As a result, they end up at the mercy of the person who is breaking the rules, or perhaps another way to say it is that they end up at the mercy of the person who is playing by a *different set* of rules.

This is exactly the issue horse people run into when they are around horses. Horses play under one set of rules, the ones dictated by the laws of nature, and humans play under another set of rules, the ones designed by man. It is for that reason that humans are so often surprised by the things horses do, especially when it involves the human getting injured. Because we have been lulled into a state of complacency regarding our own personal safety, we often have a hard time believing that something or someone would actually try to harm us, whether intentionally or accidentally. As a result, we end up inadvertently putting ourselves in danger, and then keeping ourselves in the role of the victim, and looking for ways to solve problems *after* they have already occurred.

———————

Many years ago I was invited to go to Holland to do a series of clinics just outside the city of Amsterdam. We had a couple days off between the first and second clinic, and so my interpreter asked if I'd like to travel into Amsterdam to do some sightseeing. Up until then, basically all I had seen of the country was the airport and the inside of an arena, so I jumped at the chance to go have a look around.

My interpreter, April, drove us relatively close to the city where we parked at a train station and took the train into the middle of town, instead of driving into the city and trying to find a place to park. While on the train, she mentioned in passing to be mindful of pickpockets and muggers, as crime in the city at the time was pretty high, particularly after dark and especially when it came to tourists.

The only precaution I took after she mentioned that was taking my wallet from the back pocket of my jeans and placing it in my front pocket. Other than that, I wasn't overly concerned, and once in the city, we spent the day going to all the typical tourist attractions, had lunch at a little café, took a boat ride through the canals, and had dinner on the patio of a nice Italian restaurant. It had been a very relaxing day and we had a lot of fun looking around and getting a feel for the city. However, on the way back to the train station that evening, which was a good two-mile walk from the restaurant, I began to get a strange feeling. I couldn't help but sense that we were being watched, and because of it, from time to time I would nonchalantly glance around to see if I could notice anything out of the ordinary.

It was just after dark and while the streets were still fairly full of people, the foot traffic had thinned quite a bit since earlier in the day. The first time I looked around I didn't really see anything that I would consider unusual. Still, I couldn't shake the feeling we were being watched, and by the third time I glanced around, I saw them—two young men in their late teens or early twenties that I actually remembered seeing several times throughout the day. One was small and thin, with greasy long dark hair and the other was about my size, also thin with dirty short blond hair.

I remembered seeing the pair near the café where we had lunch, then again by the home of Anne Frank that we'd visited. They were standing on a bridge we had gone under while on our boat ride, they'd also walked past the Italian restaurant several times, and now, they were following us as we made our way back to the train station. Each time we stopped to look in a shop window, they would stop. If we crossed the street, so would they. If we crossed back, they would follow. April had also noticed them, and instinctively, I guess, she brought her purse closer to her body and held it tight with both hands.

There was a large open square near the train station bustling with people, and as we entered the square, I looked back to see the two men closing in on us rather quickly. Up until then they had never gotten any closer than about a half a block, but now it was clear that whatever they were planning; it was going to happen in this square. I would find out later from April that many of the muggings in the city would happen in this square where tourists would get accosted, give up their valuables, and the muggers would just disappear into the crowd.

I had no idea what, if anything, these two men were up to. Regardless, I made up my mind right then and there I wasn't going to act like a victim, and as they began to close in us, I stopped, turned and made direct eye contact with them. I said nothing but made my intent very clear . . . regardless of what their plans were, April and I were to be left alone. The men stopped abruptly, nervously glanced around, then turned and quickly made their way over to another part of the square where a young lady was playing an old and apparently abandoned upright piano. April and I both stood and watched them all the way to the piano, where they finally disappeared into the crowd.

I realize now that I didn't really have a plan as to what I would have actually done if they had pushed the issue. I guess that wasn't important at the time. What was important was that I created a confident and determined presence, much like I would when working with an unruly horse. I wanted them to know that I was in control of the situation—whether I actually was or not didn't really matter. Most of the time just creating a presence is enough to head off potentially troublesome situations like this, whether working with animals or with people.

In another instance just recently, I was walking my dog, Ring, a little but very energetic Border collie, around the small lake we have in the middle of our town. The path around the lake is about four miles long, and about three quarters of the way around, I noticed a small woman leading a big dog down near the water. The dog caught a glimpse of Ring and immediately turned and ran toward her, pulling the small woman along with him. He charged up the bank, his hackles raised, and barking and growling menacingly. "Duke, no!" his owner shouted repeatedly as she was dragged helplessly along behind.

Without thinking, I turned toward the dog and, again, creating the same presence I use with an unruly horse, moved directly at him. Ring was off leash at the time, so I took the end of the leash I was holding with the snap attached and began swinging it in the direction of the charging dog, just as I would if it were the end of a lead rope. There was no emotion involved, just very direct communication. My intent was clear. I was going to protect myself and I was going to protect my dog and I wasn't going to be harmed while I was doing it.

The dog stopped dead in his tracks just a few feet from where I was standing, tucked his tail, and quietly moved a couple steps back, finally putting some slack in his leash. He gave one last woof, and again, I took a step toward him. He moved another step back, and as he did, his ears, head, and hackles began to drop. Like the men in Amsterdam, it was clear the dog had changed his mind about what he had planned on doing, so I turned without a word, as if nothing had even happened, and Ring and I continued on our way. It was only after everything was all over that I noticed Ring had tucked herself in behind me, and during the entire episode, she had made no attempt to run or even defend herself.

Again, I wanted my intent to be unmistakable and decisive. I did not want that dog to have to question what I was saying to him, and in order for that to happen, it meant that I couldn't question what I was saying, either. I was determined and clear, and for me, I believe it is that clarity of thought that more times than not will determine the outcome of such situations, whether dealing with dogs, people, or horses.

Now, before going any further, I just want to mention that the reason I bring up these two specific instances is to illustrate what I meant when I said that not everybody plays under the same rules of survival or self-protection. In both cases, the individuals involved here were playing by a different set of rules than what most people are used to dealing with. It could be argued that the men in Amsterdam, assuming they did mean us harm, and the dog by the lake were both working more off the laws of nature than they were any domestic or man-made laws.

When it comes to nature, whoever is the quickest, strongest, fastest, and most willing to do whatever it takes to survive, will survive. When it comes to the laws of man, the playing field is much more level. Everybody's chances of survival, regardless of size, strength, physical ability, intelligence, age, or social status, are more or less equal. Because we are so accustomed to being taken care of, if you will, by the laws of man, we can quickly become perplexed and confused when confronted by something or someone who is operating under a different set of laws. Even with that, however, if we can step back and try to understand the rules that those other individuals are operating under, and prepare ourselves the best way we can for such an encounter, it can give us a much better chance at responding in a positive manner when actually confronted by them.

I don't want people to misunderstand my point here. When I mention the idea of preparing ourselves for encounters with folks or animals who may be operating by a different set of rules than we are, I'm not suggesting that we need to somehow act as though we should be getting ready for battle, or live our lives in a paranoid state of hyper awareness. I am simply saying that long before we actually run into such an unpleasant situation, we could be doing a few relatively easy things that would get us ready to act in a positive, preventative, or even proactive manner should such an encounter occur.

The first, and probably most important, factor in preparing ourselves for dealing with the unexpected is learning how to breathe properly. This is such an important part of everything we do when it comes not just to working with horses but how we live our life in general, that it is one of the first things we talk about with riders in our horsemanship clinics and it is the first thing we talk about with the participants in our Aikido for Horsemen workshops as well.

Obviously, everybody is already breathing to one degree or another. The problem is most of us are only using a small portion of our lungs, and the portion we are using is the area reserved for the triggering of our fight or flight systems, the same systems our horses use whenever they feel threatened by a worrisome situation. Here's a little test we use to help people see whether they're using their entire lung, or just the portion needed to trigger fight or flight.

While stationary (either sitting or standing), we start by having folks inhaling normally then exhaling normally. We have them do that a few times, then while inhaling we ask them to feel where the air goes in their body just before they exhale again. We ask them to check if their inhale stops in their throat, upper chest, middle chest, upper stomach, or lower stomach. We then have them do this a few times to get a good feel for where the air is going in their body.

If they find their air is stopping in their throat, upper, or middle chest, the chances are very good that they are emotionally in a fight or flight mode, and if they aren't already there, they're not far from it. If their breath goes all the way to their upper or lower stomach, they are usually in a much calmer state of mind and, overall, able to handle unexpected situations much easier than someone who isn't breathing properly.

Once they've checked where their breath is going while stationary, we then have them start walking normally and see how many strides they can get to an inhale and how many they can get to an exhale without holding their breath at the end of the inhale or the end of the exhale. Most folks who don't have any health issues are usually able to comfortably get around four or five strides on an inhale and five or six on an exhale (this number should be the same when folks ride their horses in the walk as well). Anything less, and they are usually taking very shallow breaths or holding their breath, neither of which are particularly good for staying in a calm state of mind. (We also try to remind folks that however many strides they get to an inhale, they should be able to get at least one more on an exhale as people have more muscle to exhale than they do to inhale.)

If they find that their breath is short or stopping in the upper part of their body, we give them a little quick and easy exercise that they can use to help bring their breath lower and so that it fills more of their lung. We ask them to simply take both thumbs and place them on their very bottom rib on either side of their body—the little floating ribs. Then as they inhale, we ask them to try to get their thumbs to move outward without raising their shoulders and without filling their chest with air. If this is something you decide to try at home, you may want to do this in front of a mirror to make sure your chest isn't inflating or your shoulders aren't rising.

The idea here is to bring some awareness to where we want the air to travel in our body. Most of us have been breathing very shallowly for a very long time, and so changing this pattern is not always easy. In fact, it usually takes a human about twenty-one days to change a long-established pattern that they've been relying on. However, once the breathing pattern *is* changed, it will go a very long way to helping establish the other ideas that we can use to help us deal with unexpected situations.

Before going any further, I would like to mention that there is a wonderful book for those folks who are interested in finding out how to change or improve their breathing. It is called, interestingly enough, The Breathing Book, *written by Donna Farhi. I encourage all of our students to get this book as it is not only extremely informative, but it is also very easy to understand and, for most folks, easy to implement as well.*

One of the other things I believe is extremely important in dealing with horses, as well as people, is one that we have already touched on. It is creating a clear and decisive presence. Creating a presence is important not only in being able to deal with certain situations whether related to horses or people or both, but it is also important for just being able to get through life in general.

I remember reading about a study that was done at one of the federal prisons here in the United States. In this study, researches brought in one hundred inmates who had been convicted of assault and robbery. One by one the researchers showed the inmates video clips of random people walking down the street and then asked the men to pick out which individuals they would choose to attack. In nearly every case, every inmate picked the exact same individuals as the ones they would chose to go after.

In one very telling example, each of the inmates picked a man who was about six foot six inches tall and weighed some 240 pounds as one they would attack, while the same men passed on a woman who was about five foot tall with a slight build. When asked why they would have chosen to attack the man instead of the woman, each of the inmates said that there was something about the woman that told them she would be trouble while the man looked like an easy mark.

Computer analysis later showed that each of the people the inmates picked as ones they would go after were physically out of balance in some way, and appeared not to be very aware of their surroundings, thus the inmates unconsciously saw them as a vulnerable target and someone that probably wouldn't put up much of a fight if accosted. The people the inmates passed on, on the other hand, including the small woman, were much more in balance and appeared to be much more aware of their surroundings, which the inmates translated as the person being emotionally strong and thus more likely to put up a fight.

So, just like animals in nature, people too will be more likely to prey on those that appear weak and vulnerable than they will the confident and assertive. It is also for this reason that I believe horse owners that appear weak, vulnerable, or indecisive will have horses that often struggle with taking direction from them, or who appear nervous, worried, or spooky around them.

It is my belief that anybody, regardless of age, shape, size, or gender, is able to create the kind of positive presence I am referring to here. But on the other side of the coin, I also believe a lot of that presence includes the attitude or intent we bring to the picture, along with the actual physical authority we exhibit. And for me, a big part of that physical authority boils down to how well and able our bodies perform the simple everyday tasks we ask them to do.

As we get older, many of us slowly begin to succumb to all of the little aches and pains that develop in our bodies due to the injuries, both big and small, that we've acquired over the years. Often without us even realizing it, we gradually begin to lose joint mobility and function, muscle mass, and overall flexibility and agility. Some of us find that our knees, shoulders, hips, and backs begin to hurt, and as a result, we begin to get less and less active. Some of us might start putting on weight that we can't seem to lose, and before we know it, we begin to slow down or take shortcuts, both literally and figuratively.

This "slowing down" manifests itself in all kinds of different ways. For instance, instead of fixing a good meal at home, we might stop at the local fast-food place. Rather than taking the stairs, we take the elevator. We look for places to park that are close to the store door instead of parking farther away. We drive the two blocks over to our friend's house instead of walk or ride a bike. We might even take the dog for a ten-minute walk instead of twenty, thirty, or forty-minute walks . . . if we walk him at all.

Now granted, these aren't all necessarily bad things, particularly when done in moderation. However, when done on a regular basis over and over, these types of behaviors can ultimately lead to a general overall lack of what I might refer to as physical authority. In other words, we lose our authority over our own physical well-being. When this happens—when our body begins to control us instead of us controlling it—it can be very difficult to get that control back.

The good news here is that whether or not we lose control of our physical well-being is entirely up to us. It all boils down to simple choices of behavior, coupled, of course, with self-control. We can choose to let our body get the best of us, or we can choose to take control of it and begin to seek options that will bring it back in line with who we want to be and what we want to be able to do. Even if we have gotten off track, physically, we can always turn things around and begin to make better choices regardless of the age or condition of our body. The great thing here is it is never too late.

I can speak from experience on this one. By the time I was in my late twenties, my body was a physical train wreck. In high school, just some ten years earlier, I weighed around 165 pounds and was in the best shape of my life. By the time I was twenty-eight, my back, knees, and shoulders were all giving me serious problems; my weight had ballooned up to nearly 210 pounds; and I was eating a lot of fast food, not to mention that my drinking had begun to turn into a problem.

It took a while but I began to realize the path I was going down was not a beneficial one for me and I decided to consciously make some changes. Luckily the jobs I was working at the time were physical enough that I was able to lose most of the excess weight. Eventually I had both shoulders surgically repaired, I stopped drinking, and through my training in martial arts, I was forced to start using my body properly, which helped to all but eliminate my back and knee pain.

In addition to the physicality of my work with horses, today I do a full-body workout five days a week, walk between four to seven miles a day, and train in martial arts at least twice a week. I try to keep myself as limber as possible through a series of stretches that I do most every day, and I make sure I get regular chiropractic to keep my joints from locking up. I also eat healthier, seldom if ever stopping at fast-food places, and what I do eat I try to keep to smaller and more reasonable portions.

Still, I don't kid myself. I'm not as young as I once was, and I understand there are certain things I used to be able to do that I probably won't ever be able to do again. But instead of focusing on what I can't do, I choose instead to focus on those things I can do to keep myself in the best physical shape I can, and I work toward improving those things. Even at that, I am continually finding ways to change my workout and further challenge and strengthen my body, which in turn helps to strengthen and challenge my mind on a number of levels.

What many people find, once they begin to take control of their body, is that it begins to change their level of confidence in a positive way. By shedding a few of those extra pounds or being able to lift or move something they weren't able to lift or move before, they suddenly begin to feel empowered, and it is this empowerment that can eventually begin to shape and add to better overall speed and smoothness of movement, and improve balance as well as awareness of one's surroundings. And it is this improved awareness of our surroundings that ultimately helps in our own self-protection, whether just walking down the street or when working with horses.

Still, improved awareness, better physical fitness, breathing correctly, and having the ability to create a presence are nothing if we aren't willing to do something to actually protect ourselves should such a situation come up. I know of many a horse lover over the years that got run over or knocked down by a horse when it got spooked, simply because the person couldn't get out of the way in time or didn't have the wherewithal to get the horse stopped or turned before it crashed into them. There are folks out there who have been bitten and kicked because they weren't thinking of protecting themselves *before* the angry horse they were working with decided to strike out. And we all know of riders (and in fact, we may be one) who have been injured because they came off a horse and landed awkwardly.

Again, many of these things occur because we are playing by one set of rules and the horse is playing by another. Any horse, if pushed, frightened, or upset enough, is capable of protecting itself by any means necessary, regardless of their training, background, or the kind of relationship we have with them or think we might have with them. Many people, on the other hand, don't seem to feel they have the right to protect themselves when the tables are turned. I believe it's always important to keep in mind that even if a horse didn't mean to hurt us by their behavior, it doesn't make it hurt any less.

Some time back at one of our clinics, I watched helplessly as a clinic participant who was waiting her turn outside the arena was knocked over and stepped on when her horse, who had been jumping around and calling back to his buddy at the barn, mindlessly ran into her. The woman had been standing passively while her horse got more and more frantic, until he finally lost his mind and blew up, right on top of her. Later, when I asked her why she hadn't done something to direct the horse's energy or get him off of her, she said that she didn't feel she should step in because she was afraid the horse might get mad at her.

This is a perfect example of what I'm talking about. Here was a horse that was doing whatever he needed to do to try to find a way to feel better, not really caring if he ran some-one over or not, and we had an owner who would rather get run over than run the risk of having her horse be mad at her. Now I'm not saying that what she did was right or wrong, I'm simply pointing out how we humans sometimes operate by a completely different set of rules than our horses do, and how we also sometimes end up paying the price for doing so.

———————

Personally, I don't see anything wrong with stepping up and saying something to a horse that is struggling, particularly if they are getting to a point where they are becoming dan-gerous to either themselves or someone else. From my perspective, in situations like that I always think of protecting myself first, then directing the horse and working on keeping them safe second.

I have had people over the years, when I discuss this topic with them, ask me how someone like myself, who spends so much time putting the horse first, would even consider putting a horse's well-being second to my own. The answer is simple. I have just as much right, not to mention responsibility, to keep myself safe as the horse does. Just like when you're on a commercial airliner and the flight crew talk about putting your oxygen mask on before helping someone else with his or her mask. The bottom line is I can't be of much help to my troubled horse if I'm lying on the ground all broken and stepped on because I didn't protect myself when I should have.

To me, self-protection is not only a very big part of being a good leader to your horse but it is also, plain and simple, just good horsemanship. Along those same lines, focusing on protecting ourselves is not just for those times when we are working with our horse on the ground. It's also for those times when we're on our horse's back and they begin to have trouble as well.

Every year, thousands of people fall off their horses, and many of those are injured, some seriously. Contrary to popular belief, the reason so many people get hurt during a fall isn't because the horse spooked or bucked or shied or whatever. It's because the rider wasn't prepared for the landing. Most people try so hard to *not* fall off their horse; they are totally unprepared for what to do if and when they actually do fall. They simply don't know how to protect themselves *while* the fall is occurring.

Years ago I ran into some old high school friends one night, and in a stroke of genius, we all decided to go skydiving the next day. There was a place that did such things not far from where I lived at the time, so the next morning, bright and early, we all loaded up in our cars and trucks and headed for the place. Once there, we were introduced to the no-nonsense, ex-military instructor who would be teaching us the finer points of how to jump out of an airplane, which he did. However, the interesting thing was the vast majority of what we learned over the next eight hours was (A) how to get out of the plane, and (B) how to land once we got to the ground.

This was in the days before tandem jumping, so once we got out of the plane, getting to the ground safely was entirely up to us as an individual. The instructor was quite clear about all the hazards involved in jumping out of an airplane and reiterated them over and over. Basically, if we did what he told us to do, we'd survive. If not, we probably wouldn't. At the end of the day, armed with all of the pertinent information we would hopefully need to jump out of a plane and return to earth safely, we all loaded into two aircrafts and up we went.

All of us did, indeed, get out of the plane safely and back down to the ground without incident. A tribute, I suppose, to either how well we paid attention to the instructor or how scared we were not to follow his direction. Either way, the point is that during this outing, we spent eight hours learning how to handle ourselves effectively and safely during what ultimately ended up being little more than a three-minute experience. Even at that, the vast majority of those eight hours was spent on the few seconds that would be needed to get out of the aircraft, and the few seconds needed to actually make contact with the ground. When we compare this to the little amount of time horse folks spend on learning how to land safely in the event of an unscheduled dismount, we can then see why so many people become injured during a fall.

A few years back, my wife Crissi, who at the time had been training in aikido for just a couple months, had a fall from a horse. She talks of how she saw the ground coming as she fell and instinctively put herself into the forward roll she had learned and been working on during her aikido classes. She landed, rolled, and popped right up uninjured. At the time, she was considering quitting aikido because she said she felt it was too difficult for her. However, after her uneventful fall, she decided to continue her training.

During our Aikido for Horsemen workshops, one of the first things on the agenda is helping people learn how to fall and roll properly. This whole process is broken down into baby steps for the students, just as it is for new students in formal aikido classes. What surprised me about some of the students in the workshops isn't that they have trouble rolling, as that is actually quite common, but how many of the students had trouble simply getting down close enough to the mat to where they could even attempt a roll in the first place! People were so afraid of being on the ground that some of them actually froze in place just kneeling down.

By the second day, however, these same folks, with a little help and encouragement, were often able to get down and roll on the mats by themselves, and by the third day they were comfortable enough that they could actually be thrown into their rolls by either an instructor or fellow student.

We have received a number of letters and feedback from students who have taken the workshops and who said, after working on their falls and rolls, that they experienced a marked improvement in their confidence when on their horse, and some even went on to begin formal aikido training once back at home. Others went so far as to buy mats of their own so they could work on their rolls at home, and still others have contacted us to tell us they actually had a fall from a horse following the workshop, and the information they learned about protecting themselves during a fall kept them from injuring themselves.

Now I must admit, growing up around horses, I never gave a second thought as to how I was supposed to land if I ever came off one. In fact, I never really gave any thought to falling off at all. I guess I just always assumed I would stay on. But of course the older one gets, the more reality begins to sink in, and looking for ways how *not* to get hurt suddenly seem to take on a little more importance.

In the horse world, some of us often give so much thought to trying to find quiet and effective ways of getting along with our horses, we seldom discuss what to do when things don't go as planned, and as a result, we often aren't prepared when they do go wrong. As I mentioned in the beginning, self-protection is an extremely important part of nature . . . perhaps *the* most important part. It's also a very important part of horsemanship.

Now I realize I haven't given many specifics here on how one should, or could, protect him or herself in the event of some kind of horse-related incident, and to be honest, I'm not sure I could. I think most horse folks, just like most martial artists, understand that each situation is always different and trying to say that if A occurs, you should always do B would seem a little silly. All the martial arts training in the world can't prepare us for every possible unexpected situation that could ever occur. However, understanding certain principles (whether in horsemanship or in martial arts) can allow us to think or act on our feet and cannot only give us a better-than-average chance at coming out of an unexpected situation unharmed, but they can also help us to get a better feel and understanding of what I would consider to be the true nature in horsemanship.

So rather than trying to discuss specific situations, their causes, and our potential responses, I think it might be better to discuss the principles that I have found most important, which apply across the board, whether in martial arts, horsemanship, or life. Specifically the principles I am talking about include the use and understanding of pressure, orientation, movement, and—quite possibly the single most essential principle—the importance of distance and/or spacing.

For me, developing a deeper understanding of these principles over the years has made a big difference in the way I see and work with horses. My hope is that as we go forward, you will find them helpful to you as well.

Chapter 5
Pressure, Part 1

———————————

Several years ago while in between riders at a clinic I was doing overseas, a woman in the audience raised her hand and asked my opinion on the idea of *natural horsemanship*. I don't know if any other clinicians or trainers get this type of question, but it was one I'd gotten a number of times at a number of different places I've been. I'm pretty sure my opinion on the matter would not fit what most folks—particularly people who had already formed a positive opinion of the idea of natural horsemanship—would like to hear. As a result, I would usually just dance around the question or politely change the subject so as to avoid some kind of unnecessary debate or potential argument on the matter.

This time, however, my attempts to deflect the topic to something else met with resistance, and anytime I tried to bring up another subject, the woman would return to her original question.

"I for one," she undauntedly said, following one such attempt at deflection, "would appreciate hearing your views on the subject of natural horsemanship. I'm sure there are others here who would be interested in them as well."

It was clear by the reaction from the people in attendance that this time, I wasn't going to be able to change the subject. I paused for what seemed like a long time before finally deciding it might be as good a time as any for people to know where I stood on the subject.

"Would you really like my honest opinion?" I asked.

"Of course."

"Well," I started. "The first thing I'd say about natural horsemanship is, I don't believe there is such a thing. Seems to me once we put a horse in an enclosure of any kind, regardless of its size, the horse is no longer in a natural state. As a result, anything we do with them past that point can't really be natural for them." A slight but noticeable rumble went through the crowd. "Now, with that being said, I would also say that I believe I've seen more damage done to horses in the name of something being 'natural' than almost any other training style or discipline out there."

The rumble got considerably more audible.

"How can you say that?" a different woman asked. "Natural horsemanship is a much kinder way of working with horses than any other way."

"Natural horsemanship is *touted* as a much kinder way," I said. "That doesn't necessarily mean it always is." My better judgment told me to stop there. But I didn't.

"Over the years," I went on, "I've seen horses that had been nearly run to death in round pens because their owner wanted to teach the horse 'respect' in the name of natural horsemanship, or wanted to teach it how to be caught in a more natural way, or they wanted to teach the horse how to look at them or come to them. I've seen horses with noses and jaws raw and bleeding by the improper use of 'natural' rope halters. I've seen horses so lame they couldn't walk because the owner insisted the horse go barefoot because doing so was supposed to be natural. There are thousands of horses all over the world that can't steer because their owners have laterally flexed them to the point where the horse's head has become disconnected from its body because some say its supposed to be a 'natural' way of softening the horse." I paused. "Heck, there were three horses at this clinic alone that had that problem."

For those folks out there who perhaps aren't familiar with the idea of lateral flexion, basically what happens is the rider sits on the horse's back and turns the horse's head, flexing its head and neck to the right and left over and over until the horse will flex in both directions with little or no effort on the rider's part. The problem with the idea is that when done in excess (which it usually is), it can, and often does, cause the horse to "disconnect" its head from its body. In other words, instead of the horse's body following its nose when it moves, like it would normally do on its own, it becomes as if the horse's head is no longer even attached to its body. When this happens, the horse usually loses its ability to steer and stop, and even when just standing still with a rider on its back, the horse will often stand with its head turned toward the rider's boot. In other words, hyper flexing the horse's neck laterally eventually becomes the horse's default behavior and any time they become frustrated or don't know what to do next, they will simply start flexing left and right.

The first three horses we'd seen in the clinic that day fell into this group. All three couldn't walk a straight line with a rider on their back because their owners, all practitioners of "natural horsemanship," had spent so much time laterally flexing their horses' necks that the horses no longer thought they should follow their own nose. All three horses seemed to have necks that looked like they were made of rubber, and we spent most of each of their sessions doing little more than working on trying to reconnect the horse's head to its body.

"On the other end of the spectrum," I continued, perhaps unadvisedly, "there are other riders out there who simply refuse to use any pressure whatsoever to help their horse learn whatever it is they want them to know because they feel the use of pressure doesn't fit under the umbrella of being 'natural.'" I paused again. "I don't know how many horses I've seen that can't turn, stop, or back up when being ridden simply because their owner doesn't believe in using pressure. I don't know how many other owners I've seen get run over by their horse because they refuse to use enough pressure to effectively teach their horse boundaries."

"Using pressure is cruel!" a voice from the crowd shouted.

"The use of pressure is natural." I smiled. "The uneducated *excess* use of pressure isn't. There is a *big* difference."

I've been surprised over the years at the sheer number of horse folks out there that either shy away from or completely refuse to use any kind of pressure when working with their horses because of this idea that the use of pressure isn't natural. The majority of these folks, or at least the ones I've run into, are admittedly heavily involved in the "natural horsemanship" movement, but others are people who, for one reason or another, have just decided they simply don't want to use pressure with their animal. Many of these people have gravitated to a type of training known as positive reinforcement, or clicker training, while others, because of their refusal to use pressure, often end up giving their horses so much leeway that their horse appears spoiled, unruly, and even dangerous because of their lack of boundaries or lack of simple understanding of basic rules when around people.

After talking with many of the folks out there that don't want to use pressure when working with their horse, I have come to believe that the main reason most avoid the use of pressure isn't so much because it bothers the horse, because when used properly, it usually doesn't, but rather because it bothers the person. In other words, the person doesn't like the way *they* feel when they use pressure. Usually it boils down to the person not knowing how much pressure to use or when to use it, or (and this is almost always the real cause) the person has a hard time using pressure without getting angry or feeling bad in some other way. They somehow associate using pressure with being confrontational, and because many folks don't do well with confrontation, they simply avoid it at all costs, whether with other people, their kids, dogs, horses, or whatever.

Still other horse people don't use pressure because they've perhaps seen trainers or other horse people either using too much pressure, which causes undue stress and anxiety for the horse, not to mention the occasional physical or emotional injury that this type of handling can cause, or (on the other end of the spectrum) they may have seen a trainer riding or working horses and getting responses from the horse with what seems like little or no pressure whatsoever. Some of these latter trainers might even ride bridleless and bareback, giving some people the impression that not only are these things easy to achieve but also quite desirable. To the inexperienced (and sometimes even the experienced) horse person, this type of thing often looks so effortless that it would appear anyone could do it, no matter the level of skill or training either the rider or the horse possess.

I have gotten the impression over the years that this overall and general lack of understanding for the proper use and application of *productive* pressure during training gets some people thinking or perhaps even expecting that either (A) they shouldn't need to use pressure at all, or (B) horses will somehow automatically respond to our good intentions without us having to use any other form of physical motivation.

However, the problem is that without either the person or the horse understanding how to use or respond to pressure properly, what often ends up transpiring is confusion, frustration, and hard feelings on the part of both individuals. In other words, not wanting to use productive pressure when working with horses is a little like a carpenter trying to build a house without understanding or even trying to use a tape measure, hammer, or saw. He might eventually be able to get the walls up, but whether or not they stay up is a matter of debate. The way that I look at it, a craftsman who not only understands his tools, but also how to use them properly, will always have more options available to him than the craftsman who doesn't. And the best way for someone to develop a keen understanding of the tools they need to use in order to improve or hone their craft is to practice with them over and over until the tool and its use simply become part of the craftsman.

———————

We were doing a clinic in Southern California, and it had been cloudy all day. Just as I finished asking the woman who sat quietly on her gelding, a sorrel quarter horse with no markings whatsoever, what she wanted to work on, tiny puffs of dust began rising from the arena floor as the occasional drop of rainwater landed in the dry sand.

"My horse doesn't turn very well," she said. "He doesn't stop or back up, either."

"Ever?" I questioned.

"Not really," she replied. "Sometimes he does, and sometimes he doesn't." She shrugged. "I guess it just depends on how he feels."

"Well," I said, "Could you show me what he does when you ask him to back up?"

The woman picked up her reins, and without even making contact with the nice leather side pull her horse was wearing, she sat patiently waiting for the horse to move. (For those who may not be familiar with a side pull, it is simply a leather headstall, very similar in looks to a flat nylon or leather halter, without a bit. In place of the bit, the reins are attached to rings on ether side of the horse's face, near his cheeks.)

As expected, there was no response from the horse whatsoever, and other than an occasional flinch from a raindrop hitting near his eye, he looked as though he was ready to take a little nap.

"Is this what he does?" I asked.

"Usually." She shrugged, slowly letting go of the reins.

"Is that how much pressure you normally use when you ask him to back?"

"I'm not supposed to use pressure," the woman said, meekly.

"You're not?"

"I've been working with a trainer who told me I have terrible hands," she said. "She told me I couldn't use a bit with my horse because it would ruin his mouth, and until I could learn how to be better with my hands, I wasn't supposed to make contact with the side pull either."

At first, I wasn't sure if the woman was joking or not. After all, I'd worked with a lot of folks over the years who had abandoned using a bit with their horse either because someone told them their hands were too harsh or they felt, on their own, that their hands were harsh and that they didn't want to hurt their horse's mouth. But I'd never heard of someone having been told to abandon the use of pressure altogether, and then be expected to somehow get better at using it. It just didn't make sense to me.

Apparently, it hadn't made sense to the rider either because when I asked her what she had been doing to try and improve her feel through the reins, she said she hadn't really known what to do. She said her trainer, who she'd been with for over a year, wasn't giving her any ideas on how to improve either.

"If you're not working on this in your lessons," I questioned, "then what *are* you doing?"

"Mostly I just sit around and watch my trainer ride my horse." She shrugged.

"Okay," I said. "If that's the case, then I would imagine your horse will be fairly responsive by now, so now it's just a matter of getting you and him on the same page."

"How are we going to do that?"

"By teaching you how to be better with your hands."

"But how?"

I smiled. "Well, the first thing we're going to do is have you pick up your reins and make some contact. Then . . ."

"But I'm not supposed to do that." The woman said, almost apologetically.

"I understand." I nodded. "But the only way your hands are going to get better is if you use them."

"I'm sure you're right," the woman agreed. "But when I told my trainer I was coming to this clinic, she made me promise to tell you that I was not supposed to use my hands on this horse under any circumstances."

"And you have told me," I acknowledged. "But let me ask you this. Does this horse belong to you, or her?"

"Well, he belongs to me, but . . ."

"And I'm assuming you've come here so you can improve your skills as a rider. Is that right?"

"Yes."

"Okay then. What we're going to do is see if we can help *you* become a better rider for *your* horse. In order to do that, I'm going to need you to pick up your reins and make contact with him."

The woman had a look of nervousness on her face.

"Don't worry," I joked. "If we need to, I'll give you a note that says it was okay for you to this."

The woman smiled.

With that, we set to the business of helping her understand and ultimately be able to use pressure to help communicate with her horse. We began very simply by establishing a scale on which to rate the pressure she was feeling at any given time, with 0 being no pressure and 10 being more than she would ever want to use. Then with her holding one end of the reins and me holding the other, we worked together on getting a feel for each of the numbers on the scale. Slack in the reins was a 0, very slight pressure was a .5, slightly above that was a 1, and so on all the way up to 10.

Once we had done that, I asked her to pick up the reins and ask her horse to back up. After she applied ever so slight contact, and seeing that her horse was not responding, I asked her how much pressure, on our new scale, she was using. "Point five, or one," she replied.

"Okay, let's increase to a one and a half," I said. And she did. Her horse began moving his head a bit, but didn't move his feet. When the movement in his head stopped we waited a second or two, then I asked her to increase the pressure to a two, which she did. This time, the horse moved his head a bit, then after just a couple more seconds, slowly and quietly, began to back up. I asked her to keep her hands as quiet and still as possible, and as he moved, he began to give himself small releases from the pressure she was applying. He took several steps before I asked her to release the pressure completely, and when she did, the horse stopped backing.

"There." I nodded. "That wasn't so bad, was it?"

"Is it always that easy?" she smiled.

"Not always," I said. "But it's a good place to start."

We then began helping her understand the idea of using contact and pressure through the reins without pulling, a concept that can be difficult for even seasoned horse people to understand, but one that I have found to be extremely important in helping both horse and rider move toward softness. The example I use quite often is how if we were to tie a rope to a post set in the ground, and then pull on the rope as hard as we could, we would feel a great deal of pressure. However, it wouldn't be the post that was applying the pressure, but rather the pressure we felt would be coming from us pulling on the stationary post. Yet if we were to move even a fraction of an inch toward the post, we would feel an immediate and fairly substantial release from that pressure.

Now while there are actually very few times when working with horses that we would want to be as rigid as a post set in the ground, the idea of using pressure without pulling is actually a fairly similar concept. If a horse were to pull on a post, the post would not pull back, it would just be there as a point of resistance, which is how I look at the use of pressure. When a horse goes toward a point of resistance instead of away from it, the horse always gets a clear and decisive release. Because of this, and over time, the horse would learn that when it applied pressure to itself by pulling on the point of resistance, it could also get a release by going *toward* that same point of resistance.

So the bottom line is that when using the reins, the less we pull, the easier it is for the horse to find a release. The more we pull, the less likely the horse will be to find a release, and thus the more bracey a horse is likely to become. After all, if a horse doesn't get a release for giving to pressure, then there isn't really any reason for them to give in the first place. But this is where people sometimes get a little confused. You see, many horse people immediately associate applying pressure (through the reins) with pulling. In other words, they feel the only way one *can* apply pressure is to pull. And that just isn't the case. The way I look at it, applying pressure is more about setting achievable boundaries for both you and your horse than it is about trying to force the horse to do something.

Something happened a few years back that, for me, really illustrates this idea of what an achievable boundary might look like and feel like. While traveling cross-country for a series of clinics in the Midwest, we stopped at a friend's place in Iowa to overnight with our horses. They had just enclosed their entire property, including the two-acre pasture our horses would be staying in for the night, with fencing material known as ElectroBraid. This particular material looks somewhat like bungee chord with very thin, almost hairlike wires twisted into the chord, which can then be electrified. The fence itself is extremely durable and is designed to give but not break if a horse should happen to run into it.

And run into it was exactly what one of our horses did. Two of the horses we were traveling with had been in this pasture in the past during another stop we had made there while traveling, and knew where the fence line was. The third was a horse that was new to us, and so it was his first time in this particular pasture. It was already dark by the time we arrived, and while our friends had the yard lights on, which illuminated the pasture to some degree, it was by no means bright. As we turned the trio into the pasture, they all almost immediately bolted for the other end of the enclosure in an effort to stretch their legs from the thirteen-hour trailer ride they had been on that day.

In seconds they had reached the far end of the pasture, turned, and raced back. As they neared the fence which held the gate we had just brought them through, our two horses that had previously been in this pasture slowed slightly in preparation for stopping before hitting the fence, but the third didn't. The big red dun gelding we had named Scooter blew past the other two and hit the ElectroBraid fence going full speed.

The impact stretched the fence five or six feet from its original position, but true to its marketing information, it didn't break. Instead, all of Scooter's energy was quickly absorbed by the fence, which slowed him to a dead stop due to the fence being stretched to its maximum stretching point. Then, almost as quickly as Scooter hit the fence, just as quickly it shot him back into the pasture unharmed.

Now for years I had been talking to people about using pressure without pulling, or in other words, setting a clear boundary with one's hands so that the horse can learn how to work softly within that boundary. The thing about this incident that really hit home for me about pressure and boundaries was the way the fence moved as Scooter ran into it. For just a brief second or two he had successfully moved the boundary, but in doing so, he put a tremendous amount of pressure on *himself*. In other words, the fence didn't apply the pressure, but rather he put pressure on himself by leaving the boundary the fence provided. Eventually, the pressure was too much, and he ended up going back inside the boundary.

What *didn't* happen was the fence didn't follow him back into the pasture, but rather it simply stopped at its original boundary line. This had been exactly the idea that I've been trying to pass along to people when I ask them to use pressure but not pull! The fence line was the boundary, just as the rider's hands become the boundary when making contact with a horse's bit. When a horse pushes, braces, or leans on the bit (for instance) he might move into the boundary, but like the fence, the farther outside that boundary the horse travels, the more pressure he would feel. The closer to the boundary he gets, the less pressure he feels. Once back inside the boundary, he would theoretically feel little or no pressure at all.

However, the only way this can realistically occur is if the rider isn't pulling on the reins, which very simply means our hands shouldn't move toward us once we have established that boundary. The horse can pull on us all he wants . . . we just shouldn't pull back.

It was this concept that I began to help the woman with during the clinic, and within just a few minutes, both her and her horse had begun to get the hang of it. Using this idea, their stops and turns became much softer and the horse became much more responsive overall. Even so, the woman was still struggling with the idea of using pressure to help her horse respond to her requests. She, like so many other folks, had been convinced by others that pressure is a bad thing and shouldn't be used under any circumstances when working with horses.

Yet everything on earth is, in some way, shape, or form, dealing with pressure every second of every day. Not only is pressure the element that holds us all securely to the earth, but all living creatures—whether a mammal being pushed through the birth canal or a bird, alligator, turtle, or other hatchling breaking out of its shell for the first time—begin their lives by responding to pressure during the birthing process. Pressure is also what forms our weather patterns, molds our rivers and streams, created and continues to create our landmasses, and even changes the shape of those landmasses. In reality, pressure is one of the most common influences found in nature and is the one thing most species not only understand but also instinctively respond to in one way or another.

Not long ago, I had the opportunity to watch a small band of wild horses as they moved across their rangelands. The herd moved along at a relatively slow walk, mares and babies out front, the stallion at the rear. As they moved along, the stallion ever so gently reached out with his nose and nudged a three-day-old baby that was falling a little behind its mother. The baby immediately trotted back up to its mother and continued along with the herd.

Just a few minutes later, after the herd had stopped to graze, the stallion and his lead mare were grazing together in a small patch of green grass when another younger mare ventured in too close to them. The stallion pinned his ears at the encroaching mare, but she didn't respond. He pinned his ears and raised his head in her direction. Still no movement from the mare. He stepped toward her, but she didn't budge. Finally, he charged, taking a bite out of her hindquarters, and she finally turned and ran. About a half hour later, the same scenario with the same players took place. The stallion and the lead mare were grazing together, and the young mare came in too close. This time, when the stallion pinned his ears, the young mare turned and walked away.

When horses use pressure with each other, as was the case with the stallion and his herd, they generally only use enough to get the job done. If one horse needs another to move out of the way, the first horse may do so by using nothing more than a simple glance. But that glance will quickly escalate to something much more if the second horse didn't move on the quieter request. It all depends on how willing the second horse is to respond. But even then, usually as soon as the second horse has moved an appropriate distance, the request stops, and both horses go back to being as quiet as they were before everything began. In most cases, neither will use an unnecessary amount of energy, and seldom will the first horse use more pressure than the situation required, even though the amount of pressure may seem to us almost nonexistent—on one end of the spectrum—and on the other end perhaps overly excessive.

Of course I am talking here primarily about horses that use "normal" pressure during their average, everyday activities and not the random, and sometimes unnecessary, use of pressure often seen used by the "alpha" horse in domestic herds.

I used to think that horses were born with an innate understanding of how to use pressure effectively, and to be honest, I still think that is the case to some degree. However, over the years, I have also come to understand that in order to become adept at it, horses seem to practice their skill at using as well as responding to pressure from an early age. It begins when they are newborns, often learning how to respond to their mother's guidance toward the teat so they can suckle. They also learn how much pressure to use in order to bring the milk down by pressing their nose into the mare's udder. Later, they learn how to move away from pressure other adolescents and adults use with them, or how to move others using pressure of their own.

Within a very short period of time, it seems, horses quickly become masters in the subtleties and nuances of the use of pressure. Personally, I believe this is because they don't have any emotion attached to it like many humans do. For horses, like so many other animals, the use of pressure isn't right or wrong or good or bad. It's simply one form of communication ultimately necessary for survival. Because horses don't attach any stigma to the use of pressure, they can practice applying it and responding to it in a more matter-of-fact way, which I believe helps to streamline the process and ultimately *allows* them the skills they need to understand it effectively. These are also skills that only get better as the horse gets older and develops more practical experience.

As a result, it is not uncommon to watch as the amount of pressure horses use with each other seems to be the exact amount needed to get the job done, and the timing of the release also seems exactly correct. I believe this is because horses have an innate understanding of something us humans struggle with when it comes to using pressure. That is that *subtleties* of communication through pressure can only occur when we understand the full effects that *all* levels of its use provide. By understanding the full effect of excessive use, as well as subtle use, it then becomes much easier for any individual to know how much pressure to use in any given situation.

Perhaps it would help to take a look at all of this from a slightly different angle. If we look at this from a martial arts standpoint, we might find that most experienced martial artists, regardless of discipline, will tell you that they don't train in their art so that they can get good at fighting, they train so that they don't have to fight. In other words, martial artists train for years and even decades so that they might develop a very deep and profound understanding of skills and techniques they hope to never use.

This is a somewhat different way of looking at their chosen art than the way some folks might look at horsemanship. While the martial artist trains hard to get better at the necessary techniques and skills their art requires, even though many of those techniques might be physically and emotionally difficult for them, many horsemen, on the other hand, often tend to avoid the things that might be emotionally and physically difficult for them (or their horse), and as a result, they simply never get better at them.

Helen Keller once said that, "Character cannot be developed in ease and quiet. Only through experience of trial and suffering can the soul be strengthened, ambition inspired, and success achieved." My aikido instructor, Shihan Eric Adams, may have said it a little more concisely when he mentioned one day in class that "when we only practice the things we're good at and stay away from the things that are difficult, the things that are difficult never get easier."

I have had a number of people over the years tell me that one of the reasons they don't like using pressure with their horses is because when they do use it, it doesn't get the desired response from the horse, or have the desired effect. I must say, I completely understand where these folks are coming from. I remember when I first began my martial arts training, my techniques seldom, if ever, had the desired response or effect on my partner that I was looking for. However, over time and with continued practice and a great deal of trial and error, eventually I developed better understanding, better body control, and better self-control. It was only then that the desired responses and effects of the techniques began to come through. Not only that, but as my skill at applying the techniques grew, the amount of muscle I originally felt I needed to get the techniques to be effective began to drop dramatically.

Still, getting better at a technique or skill, whether in horsemanship or any other art, isn't just about continuous repetition, although that can be and often is helpful. Even more important during training is each individual student's ability to step back and take note of the effect the technique or skill had once it had been applied. Whether the effect was the desired one or not doesn't really matter. What does matter is that the individual is able to recognize what the effect was, and then make an adustment if necessary to get closer to where they want to be. But I suppose more to the point is that growth, understanding, and improvement can't be accomplished at all if the person has completely abandoned the technique in the first place! A martial artist will never be able to control his or her technique very well if they never practice.

I believe the use of pressure while working with horses also falls into this category. It's very difficult for a person to be able to effectively use pressure, or even understand its effects, if they refuse (for whatever reason) to use it, or are simply afraid to practice with it. If we aren't careful, using pressure then becomes the imaginary monster in the closet—one we become so afraid of that we eventually even avoid opening the door.

Chapter 6
Pressure, Part 2

The woman had been trying to lead her large gray quarter horse into the arena for ten minutes, only to have him stop dead in his tracks fifteen feet from the arena gate and refuse to move. She had tried everything she knew to get the gelding to walk forward, but he was having none of it. He had planted his feet like he grew roots and that, apparently, was that.

"So is this what you mean when you said he sometimes refuses to lead?" I asked.

"This is it," she said in exasperation. We were in the middle of the afternoon session of the first day of a four-day clinic, and this particular woman had approached me during our lunch break earlier that day to talk to me about her horse. She had explained that one of her horse's many and varied behavioral issues was that he would often suddenly stop dead in his tracks and refuse to move. Once he stopped, it was near impossible to get him moving again, unless it was back to the barn or in any other direction the horse decided he wanted to go.

She had had him worked on by an equine chiropractor, vet, and dentist to eliminate physical issues, and all three gave the gelding a clean bill of health. She had worked with him using clicker training and found that once he'd made up his mind not to move, he wasn't terribly motivated by the food treats she offered him as a reward to do so.

"Do you mind if I give it a try?" I asked.

"Be my guest," she said, handing me the horse's lead rope.

I asked the horse to move forward by applying minimal pressure to the rope, but it was as if I was trying to move a 1,300-pound rock that was tied to a tree. Maintaining a firm but soft contact on the rope, I moved around to the horse's side to see if I could get him to move his front feet. He wouldn't. I moved around to his other side, but there was no movement there either. I tried this a few more times, but the horse was completely uninterested in moving and totally locked up. In fact, he was so unresponsive that he actually appeared to be falling asleep.

"So is this pretty typical?" I asked. "Once he stops, he just refuses to move forward?"

"That's pretty much it," she said, her arms folded across her chest.

"Have you ever tried to get him to move backward when he does this?"

"Backward? No I haven't." She shook her head. "I don't want him to go backward. I want him to go forward."

"Well, maybe if we can get him going backward, we can turn it into forward." I shrugged. "How about it?"

"Go for it." She moved her hands as if she were handing me a serving tray.

With that, I asked the gelding to move forward one more time by taking up some contact on the rope. Again he refused, and this time instead of taking up more contact, I

immediately began swinging the lead rope and occasionally slapping the end of it on the ground in front of him and slightly off to the side. At first, there was no response, so I began swinging the rope with a little more vigor. This got a rise out of him, but not much of one. I swung the rope harder, slapped the end of it on the ground with more energy, and this time added making a hissing noise. This finally got a change from the horse. He immediately began backpedaling with his head high, eyes wide, and nostrils flared. He continued to move backward, and I continued to swing the rope and slap the lead rope on the ground.

After traveling some thirty or forty feet, the horse, having not gotten a release by going backward, tried going sideways. I continued to swing the rope. He swung a tight circle around me, going backward and sideways at the same time. The way he did this was by pulling backward on the lead rope while at the same time moving in a circle. I continued to swing and slap the ground with the rope. Finally, having not gotten a release for backward or sideways, the horse stopped pulling on the rope and lurched forward. At that point, I stopped swinging the rope and, at the very same time, turned and walked forward with him back toward the arena. The horse tentatively followed on a loose lead rope all the way to the exact same spot where he had stopped when his owner had been leading him. He then planted his feet again.

Again, I immediately turned toward him and began swinging the rope and slapping the end of it on the ground. Now again, I wasn't aiming the rope directly *at* or *toward* the horse, but rather off to the side and at a slight angle parallel to his shoulder. This gave him a clear opening to move forward if he so chose, which he didn't . . . at least not at first. He began his movement by once again shooting backward, although not as far as before, then again trying to go sideways, and finally forward. At that point the rope stopped, and I quietly turned and went forward with him.

This went on for about five minutes before the gelding realized stopping dead in his tracks wasn't what we were looking for. Once that happened, he followed easily and willingly for both his owner and me. Later, when we were finished with the clinic for the day, my assistant at the time—who had been with me on a semiregular basis for about three years—came to me with a look of confusion on her face.

"Can I ask a question about the way that you worked with that gray gelding earlier?" she said.

"Sure."

"Well," she started, "I must say I was a little surprised by the way you handled him."

"Oh?" I said. "Why's that?"

"I've just never seen you use that much pressure before."

"I haven't needed to." I shrugged. "Not when you were around, anyway."

"But everything you do is always so low key," she said.

"Not always," I commented. "Just most of the time."

"Most of the time?"

"Horses will always respond to the least amount of pressure," I started. "But we don't actually dictate how much that is. They do. The majority of horses you've seen me work with up until today have all told me they would respond to pressure that was on the lower end of that scale. The gray today told me he needed more, so that's what I offered him."

"I'm not sure I get it." It was clear by the look on her face that she didn't. "I've only seen you to be real quiet with horses, so I guess I thought that's all you did."

"Maybe I can put it another way. Have you ever seen the movie *Quigley Down Under*?" I asked.

"With Tom Selleck?" She smiled.

"Yeah, that's the one." I nodded. "Early in that movie, Tom Selleck's character, who is an expert rifleman, is talking with the movie's villain, a man named Marsten. In the scene, Marsten asks Selleck's character, Quigley, if he'd like to look at the Colt pistols that Marsten carries and Quigley declines, saying that he 'never had much use for one.'"

"I remember." She nodded.

"Well," I continued, "you remember how, at the end of the movie, Quigley ends up in a duel with Marsten and two of his ranch hands in which Quigley is forced to use a pistol instead of his rifle?"

"Yes."

"Okay," I nodded. "Well, in that scene Quigley outdraws and then shoots all three bad guys with three rounds from his pistol. He then walks up to the dying Marsten and says, 'I said I didn't have much use for one (referring to the pistol) . . . I never said I didn't know how to use one.'" I watched her to see if she made the connection, then went on to clarify. "Just because I don't often use a lot of pressure with horses," I said, "doesn't necessarily mean I won't or that I don't know how, particularly if a horse tells me he needs more than I would like to use."

I went on to explain that using that much pressure, while in some cases necessary, shouldn't be our first option, and it should not stay at that intensity. In other words, what I did with the gelding, and what I do in all situations when working with horses, whether the horse is willing and responsive or resistant and stuck, is start as soft as I want the horse to respond and end as soft as I want the horse to respond. The learning will take place in the middle. With the gelding, I ended up using more pressure with him than I would have liked, but I used enough to get a response so that I could direct him to what we wanted him to learn and know. I started soft and ended soft, and ultimately, he was able to figure out what we were looking for from him.

———

In a similar situation at another clinic some time later, I found myself working with a welsh pony that, over time, had taken to charging, pulling away, rearing, and striking anytime someone asked him to go anywhere or do anything he didn't want to do. This particular pony belonged to a young, but very experienced, little girl that used him primarily for jumping, a job that the pony did well and, by all accounts, seemed to enjoy. However, due to the pony's behavior, it was also something they hadn't done with him in months due to the fact they didn't feel he was safe to be around.

The pony had never been any trouble for anybody, and his unwanted behavior showed up only after the family had gone on a two-week vacation, during which time they had a neighbor tending to their horses. The dramatic change in the pony's behavior was apparent as soon as they returned home, and when the girl's mother asked the neighbor what happened during their absence that might have caused the behavior, the neighbor would only say the behavior showed up a few days after the family left and it had gotten worse the longer they were gone.

By the time they brought the pony to the clinic, the behavior had gotten increasingly more animated and much more dangerous, and the mother was seriously considering selling the little guy in order to keep her daughter safe—something nobody wanted to do. After watching the mother lead the pony into the arena, it became clear that the problem was already almost out of control, and the behavior was indeed dangerous. No less than three times from the gate to the arena, the pony had charged toward her, teeth bared. He also had reared and struck at the woman several times, one time grazing her bicep, and when he wasn't rearing and striking or charging, he was trying to bolt away from her. To her credit, the woman not only acted calm and was reassuring to the little horse but also gave him pretty consistent and relatively positive direction as well.

Still, the pony was having none of it, and it became clear that if we were to help him change the way he was feeling, we were not only going to need to help him figure out how to go forward when someone asked, but we also had to help him find a way to change his mind about the potentially dangerous behavior he was already exhibiting and turn it into something much more constructive.

I worked with this horse in a relatively comparable way to the big gray horse I spoke about earlier, with the exception that with this guy, I needed to do everything much quicker, and I needed to give him much more focused and clear direction. This particular horse's behavior was much more ingrained in him than was the gray gelding's behavior, and so it took a little more time to get him thinking differently and ultimately acting in a more productive and safe way. Still, within about a half hour, the pony was following quietly when being led and no longer offering the rearing, bolting, or striking that was so frequent when he first came into the arena.

The last thirty minutes of the pony's session that day was spent with both the woman and her daughter working with him and learning how to direct the behavior if it showed up again, which he really didn't seem too interested in doing anymore. When all three left the arena, the woman told me the pony's behavior was the best it had been in months and that they felt good about the fact that it appeared they had their quiet little pony back.

Now I'm not relating this story because of the end result or to talk about the specifics of how we helped the pony feel better, but rather I relate the story because of a question (which actually started out more as a statement) asked by an auditor at the end of the session.

"You used a lot of pressure on that pony." The thin, balding man said after raising his hand.

It was an interesting statement. While there was no question that there had been times when I did have to use more pressure with the pony than I would have liked, overall, I felt he hadn't required as much pressure as I would have thought, considering how troubled he was. As a result, I felt I had done much more directing of the pony than actual application of pressure.

"Would you be interested in learning a better way to work with a horse that wouldn't take *any* pressure?" he then asked.

My first thought following the question was that this fellow must either be a follower or practitioner of positive reinforcement. Positive reinforcement is a popular method of training all kinds of animals from dolphins and whales to house cats, dogs, and horses. Simply put, it is a method in which, when done properly, the animal only experiences the positive effects of training and supposedly never experiences any negative effects. Usually this type of training is done by using food rewards for desired behaviors that the animal willingly offers up rather than using pressure of any kind to help direct the animal toward the desired behavior. It can be a very effective way of working with animals, as food is a very strong motivator for the vast majority of animals on the planet, although it is not the strongest motivator.

"Sure," I said, answering the man's question. "As long as it was effective and didn't cause any more confusion than the horse is already experiencing."

The man then launched into a very detailed explanation of positive reinforcement that sounded like it was going to get quite lengthy. So before he got too far into it, I stopped him and asked if instead of going into it right then and there, he would e-mail me with the specifics of what he was going to talk about so I could look it over when I had time on my own, as opposed to using the next rider's time for discussing it, to which he agreed.

A few weeks later, and true to his word, he e-mailed me with his thoughts on why positive reinforcement should not only have been used on the little welsh pony but also why it should be used to train or retrain all horses regardless of the types of behavioral issues they might exhibit. His was not the first such e-mail or discussion I had had with proponents of positive reinforcement training in which the person felt *all* horses should be trained with the method. I have actually been involved in quite a number of such discussions over the years. His was just the lengthiest.

I say his was the lengthiest because his first e-mail to me on the subject was some ten pages long, and his second was even longer. He was quite passionate about the subject and while he had admittedly only been practicing the technique for a short time, he had definitely been spending a lot of time researching it. Still much of what he said and wrote about on positive reinforcement in his e-mails was nothing new to me and were all the same arguments I had heard during every other discussion on the subject I had ever had with other practitioners and supporters.

While each of the proponents of positive reinforcement that I have talked to over the years all have their own individual reasons for using it, almost all practitioners' bottom line seems to be that they feel positive reinforcement doesn't stress the horse (or the trainer) during the training process. Each one also has been able to recount seemingly miraculous progress that they were able to make with a horse using positive reinforcement when "traditional" training methods had failed in the past.

I must admit, I agree with them on these two counts. Positive reinforcement, when done properly, is indeed a very low-stress way of working with horses—providing the horse is in a relatively low-stress frame of mind to begin with. In other words, positive reinforcement can, and often does, get sidetracked when a horse suddenly becomes worried or frightened. In fact, when fear gets involved, positive reinforcement often doesn't work at all.

Many years ago while at a large horse expo, I went to see a woman who was giving a talk on the benefits of positive reinforcement, or in this case, "clicker training," when working with horses. For the first part of her talk she discussed the mechanics, if you will, of how clicker training worked.

She said that clicker training starts with teaching the horse how to search for a specific target, such as a small cone for instance. Then, anytime the horse looks in the direction of the cone, the handler would make a sound such as a click, either with their mouth or with a small tool held between their two fingers that when pressed made a "clicking" sound. Immediately following the "click," the horse would be given a food treat as a reward for looking in the direction of the cone.

By working in such a way over time, the horse could easily be taught to not only look in the direction of the cone but, within a very short period, would actually go over and touch the cone with their nose or even pick the cone up with their teeth. She said this method of working was known as "targeting" and is the method used in training whales and dolphins that live in captivity. Once the horse understood the concept of targeting, it could then be taught any number of simple and even complex behaviors without the horse ever becoming stressed or worried.

Having spent as much time as I have trying to find ways to work *with* horses instead of against them, the idea of being able to train a horse without stressing or worrying them intrigued me. The woman then gave example after example of the number of truly troubled horses she had helped by using clicker training, and I have to admit, some of the stories she told were pretty amazing.

She then began talking about the horse she brought to work with on that day. This particular horse was one of those that had been extremely troubled when she first started working with him due to some terribly abusive handling he had had before he came to her. But now, six months later and thanks to clicker training, she could say that this once scared and even dangerous horse had been completely rehabilitated. He was not only much calmer and quieter but also extremely willing and even friendly toward people.

She sang the horse's praises for several minutes before actually bringing him out into the little twenty foot by twenty foot arena in which she was giving the demo, and during that time she made a point to mention on several occasions how she had been very careful not to stress him in any way during his training. She said by doing this, it kept the horse in a learning state of mind and allowed for the improvement that we were about to see.

I must admit, by the way she spoke about the horse, I was expecting to see a dead quiet, docile creature that was going to run flawlessly through a prerehearsed clicker training routine that she and he had previously worked out. Much to my surprise, and I think to the surprise of every one else who was in attendance that day, what came into the little arena was about as far from docile as one could possibly get. When the gate opened, in charged a big, frantic thoroughbred gelding that was snorting fire and dancing around on his hind legs.

The woman giving the demo seemed genuinely surprised at what she was seeing from the horse, but undaunted, she began to go into the routine she had been working on with the horse at home. Unfortunately, the horse was having none of it, and within just a few short minutes of him entering the arena, the woman had already been run over, stepped on, and kicked, and things didn't get much better by the end.

Now please don't get me wrong. I am not relating this story to criticize the woman or downplay the role of positive reinforcement when working with animals, particularly when done properly. Rather, the reason I bring up this specific occurrence isn't because of what the trainer had done with the horse through clicker training, but what the trainer *didn't* do with the horse. Specifically, she never allowed the horse to become stressed during his rehabilitation, and in fact (as she had mentioned several times) she had actually gone out of her way to make sure he *didn't* get stressed.

As a result, when he found himself in a situation he was unfamiliar with, like being in a strange place in a small pen surrounded by people, loudspeaker blaring, etc., he ended up being completely unprepared to handle it, and as a result, he got himself into a state of panic that he simply wasn't able to work himself out of. Unfortunately, because the woman had only focused on teaching the horse what could arguably be referred to as a series of "tricks" during their time together, instead of developing a relationship based on mutual trust, she was unable to help him when he got upset.

One of the main reasons for this is that the motivation for most positive reinforcement behavior training, including the training the woman had done with this particular horse, is food. This form of motivation works really well for training predatory animals such as dogs, dolphins, and killer whales because not only are most predators extremely food oriented, but they also aren't terribly fearful, even when placed in strange or new situations or places.

In fact, rather than a predator becoming fearful when in a new or strange place, generally their "seek" system will kick in instead. The seek system in predators not only tells them where they are and who has been there before them, but it also tells them if there's any food to be had, whether in the form of prey or in the form of carrion. Prey animals like horses, on the other hand, will often become fearful in a new or unfamiliar place or situation mostly because they are the food that the predators are looking for. Because of this and due to millions of years of evolution, fear has become the horse's strongest form of motivation—not food.

That is why some positive reinforcement-trained horses do really well in familiar situations or places but not so well in others. When out of their element, the fear drive will kick in and override the horse's hunger drive. Because positive reinforcement (at least initially) works in conjunction with food rewards, it can sometimes be very difficult for the horse to tune in to its handler under stressful situations.

Another reason positive reinforcement-trained horses sometimes have trouble in stressful situations is due to the fact that, for the most part, positive reinforcement doesn't really happen very much in nature. Perhaps another way to say that is that positive reinforcement, the way we humans see it, doesn't really exist with horses in nature. For instance, when horse A pushes horse B out from under a shade tree, horse A doesn't immediately rush over to horse B and offer it a mouthful of grass as a reward. Rather, the only reward horse B gets after moving out from under the tree is a release of pressure it felt when horse A stopped pushing.

In addition to an overall lack of positive reinforcement in the wild, horses in the wild also seldom, if ever, suddenly find themselves alone in unfamiliar or strange situations to begin with. Feral horses move into new and unfamiliar areas gradually so as not to be taken by surprise, unlike domestic horses that can easily be transported hundreds of miles in a day and then be thrust into a completely new and sometimes frightening (for them) atmosphere that they aren't emotionally prepared to deal with. In other words, the simple act of suddenly entering new and unfamiliar places or situations is not something that exists in the wild, and so as the horse has evolved, there was simply never any need for them to develop a way of dealing with that type of circumstance.

On top of that, many positive reinforcement-trained horses also lack the ability to understand how to respond to any kind of pressure because little or none has been used on them, and as a result, they sometimes end up being a little on the pushy side, or in the case of the horse at the expo, they lose complete control of themselves in stressful situations. For me, it is this overall lack of understanding about something as basic as stress management when under pressure that worries me a little about the idea of horses that are trained *exclusively* with positive reinforcement.

Of course before going any further, I guess I should point out that there are three primary sources of pressure that all living creatures are susceptible to. They are physical pressure, emotional pressure, and environmental pressure. The first one, physical pressure, is what we feel when someone or something touches us. However, it can also come just from positive or negative energy we feel from someone who is in our relative proximity and not actually physically touching us. The second, emotional pressure, is what we might feel when we are given a deadline for an important project at work, for instance, or when a friend or family member asks something of us that we are uncomfortable with, or perhaps when money to pay bills runs short one month, and so on. And the third primary source of pressure, environmental, might show up in the form of urban sprawl and all that comes with it. Floods, draught, blizzards, tornados, hurricanes, or some other natural disaster could also be considered environmental pressure.

Animals also feel and respond to the same sources of pressure that we humans experience. For instance, horses not only learn how to respond to and give physical pressure when dealing with each other, but most humans also use the concept of teaching how to give to physical pressure during a horse's domestication and training. When it comes to emotional pressure, just like people, horses can feel the pressure from many sources. However, probably the most common source of emotional pressure for domestic horses is how a horse might feel during training and when a certain request by their handler is not clear, being misunderstood, or not understood at all. And finally, in the case of environmental pressure, both wild and domestic horses are certainly susceptible to many of the same pressures we humans feel. In the case of wild horses, they are vulnerable to draught, vanishing water holes, dried-up rangelands, storms, and in some cases, predators. Domestic horses have to deal with traffic, neighborhood dogs, show rings, confinement, riding in trailers, and so on.

The bottom line when it comes to pressure is, whether human or animal, nothing and no one is immune to it, and it can come from almost anywhere. As a result, and perhaps the good news in all this is that, all animals have developed very productive ways of being able to emotionally deal with what might be referred to as *reasonable* pressures. That is, pressures that are inherent to the simple everyday act of being a resident of the earth and living in our respective environments and communities.

So, while all animals have "factory installed" mechanisms for dealing with normal everyday stress and pressures, most domestic animals (including humans) can also be *trained* to accept and deal with what we might refer to as additional, unexpected, or uncharacteristic amounts of pressures or stressors. However, in order for the horse to begin to understand how to deal with these additional pressures, they must first be exposed to them, which is difficult when the trainer refuses—for whatever reason—to do so.

Ultimately what we are doing with our horses when we begin teaching them how to accept a rider on its back, and consequently how to turn its decision making over to us, is beginning that process of exposure. By asking them to turn their decision making over to us, we are affecting all three of their primary sources of pressure—physical, emotional, and environmental. It is for this reason that I feel so strongly that we, as horse people, should take responsibility for understanding the nuances of the pressure we are using and work daily at developing the skills necessary to become proficient with its use rather than ignoring its effects altogether.

For me, the goal when it comes to the use and understanding of pressure is to one day become as skillful with its application and release as the horse is. I'd like to be able to use just the right amount of pressure to get the desired response without troubling the horse too much and have the understanding for the application to come through to the horse quickly and without resentment.

Perhaps if I can accomplish that, I will have not only learned how to become a little better horseman, but hopefully in the process, I will have learned a little something about how to become a better person as well.

Chapter 7
Orientation

_____

The big Thoroughbred gelding had been brought to the ranch to see if anything could be done for what her owner characterized as a severe case of being barn sour. It was his third day on the place, and that morning would be the first time I would get a chance to ride him. I took him out of his pen, which was about one hundred yards from the barn, and brought him down to the hitch rail area near the barn where I saddled up.

The horse's owner was pretty specific about the dramatic and often dangerous behavior this horse could offer up when you attempted to ride him away from the barn, so as I mounted up and started down the flat wooded trail, I guess I was expecting the worst. Much to my surprise, however, he left the barn area like one of our old, dead-broke trail horses and didn't look back. We quietly wound our way through the woods nearly a quarter mile without any sign of trouble whatsoever, and just as I was beginning to think perhaps the woman may have been exaggerating a little about the horse's alleged problem, it happened.

Seemingly out of the blue, the gelding suddenly bogged his head and went to bucking. He went four or five jumps forward up the trail before spinning and crashing sideways into a nearby tree. Unfazed, he threw his head up and hit an overhanging branch then jumped across the trail, spun, and ran his backside into a nearby wooden rail fence. This caused him to lurch forward, which in turn caused me to prune a few low-hanging dead branches from the tree we ran into with my left shoulder, nearly unseating me as we rushed past.

I regained my balance and tried to turn him to the left, away from the direction of the barn, but this only caused him to slam his front feet into the ground and flip his back end in the opposite direction. Once his hind feet hit the ground, his front feet left it. He reared, turned to the right, and pruned the rest of the branches from the tree that I had just hit. Lucky for me, his movement wasn't terribly athletic, and other than losing my balance when I hit the tree, I was able to stay with him pretty well. Still, I quickly found that riding him the way he was going wasn't all that much fun, and as he flung himself across the trail for the second and third time, I decided discretion might be the better part of valor.

I turned him back toward the barn and gave him his head. He ran for all he was worth all the way back, and it was only when we were nearing the barn itself that I picked up the reins and turned him to the right, around the back of the barn. He wasn't happy about it, but he did respond, and rather than going straight toward the building, we went around it, raced down the gently sloping hill and straight into the round pen at the hill's bottom. We flew around the inside of the pen nonstop for the better part of thirty minutes before the gelding finally slowed down enough for me to ask him to stop.

While he was still prancing, shaking his head, and pawing at the ground, I jumped off, pulled my tack, and left the pen. As upset as he was, I wasn't sure how much help I could be to him anyway, so instead of trying to spend time working with him right then and there, I thought I'd see if he could calm himself down a little on his own before I spent any more time with him that morning. Little did I know at the time that calming down wasn't something he was terribly interested in, and when I went to get him out of the pen a few hours later, he was only marginally calmer than when I first put him in.

I had worked with a number of "barn sour" and "buddy sour" horses in the past and had, over time, found one of the easiest ways of helping them feel better was to just allow them the time and space to work things out on their own. Time and space were two things I had plenty of there at the ranch, so the next day, I brought the gelding from his pen, led him through the arena near the barn, and placed him in a 75' × 120' pasture adjacent to and just east of the arena. The pasture was only a couple hundred feet from the barn and in plain view of all the other horses, and still, the gelding ran and paced the fence all day long, stopping only briefly from time to time to grab a bite of grass or a drink of water.

At the end of the day, with him still pacing the fence nearest the barn, I took him from the pasture and put him back in his pen. We repeated this process for the better part of a week with seemingly little progress on the gelding's part. Then when I put him in the pasture on the sixth day, he only paced the fence for half the day and grazed the rest. The next day he began grazing as soon as I put him in the pen.

The day after that, I placed the gelding in another small pasture just a little farther away. This pasture adjoined the first pasture and was still relatively close to the barn and the other horses. I figured that due to the proximity of the first pasture, the gelding would make the switch from one to the other without too much trouble. Much to my surprise, though, the gelding immediately began pacing the fence, and the pacing persisted until I went to get him at the end of the day. He continued to pace the fence for the next four days before finally settling down and grazing as soon as I put him in.

Once he was quiet in that pasture, I placed him in another one, this one considerably closer to the barn than the last two—just sixty feet away. This time when I left him, he paced the fence so frantically he actually tore all four shoes off his feet. This went on for the next four days before he finally settled in. I then placed him in a fourth pasture with the same results. Finally, when I placed him in the fifth pasture, nearly three weeks from the day when I first threw a leg over him, he walked through the gate; and as I removed his halter, he just lowered his head and went to grazing.

From that point forward, he was like a different horse. I could take him to any of the seven pastures on the ranch and leave him by himself without him having the frantic reaction he had been offering up previously. I could also ride him off by himself in any direction for any amount of time without so much as a whinny from him, much less the anxious and worried behavior that seemed to control him in the past.

For many years I had looked at this particular horse, and others like him, as just another barn sour horse that was able to eventually work though his issue by allowing him enough time to figure it out on his own. And while that was obviously what he'd done, there was something else about this horse that got me to wondering if there was more to a horse being "barn sour" or "buddy sour" than what the terms have come to imply over the years.

The thing that kept eating away at me about this particular horse was that while certainly showing the classic signs of what most horse people might refer to as a barn sour horse, I was having trouble figuring out *why* he was doing it. In other words, I could certainly understand why he would be drawn to the barn back where he lived with his owner because I'm sure the barn there had become a place of comfort for him. But I couldn't understand why he was so drawn to the barn at the ranch. After all, I had been very careful to not do anything at all with him either in or near the barn. Not only had he never even been in the building, but in fact, he had never even been within forty feet of it.

If anything, I would have thought he would have been drawn to the pen he was living in while at the ranch, the place where he was fed and where he was surrounded by other horses that lived in pens nearby. But the pen didn't seem to have any draw for him whatsoever. I could take him from the pen without so much as him even looking back, and when I would return him to his pen at the end of the day, he would go back quietly and never be in any particular rush.

Something else I couldn't figure out was why he had so much trouble moving from one pasture to another, even though the other horses and the barn were in plain sight and even though in some cases, when moving from one pasture to the next, it actually got him closer to the barn, not farther away. Common sense would say that if he were so set on getting back to the barn, that once closer, he would be somewhat calmer. But instead, getting him closer actually seemed to get him even more upset.

This particular situation was one of those things that sort of ate at me over the years. Not in a big way, mind you, but rather just every once in a while. I would go years without thinking about it at all, then one day it would just pop back into my head, and I'd find myself going over all the details of what the horse had done and wonder why he did it in the first place.

It wouldn't be until many years later, when training with my aikido partner one night in class, that something happened that gave me a completely different perspective on what might have been at the heart of the gelding's *real* issue.

It was the fifth class in three weeks in which we would be working on the technique known as *ikkyo*. Ikkyo (pronounced *eek-yo*) is one of the most basic techniques in aikido, and it's often one of the very first techniques a new student learns. In fact, ikkyo literally means "first technique." Not surprisingly, it is also one of the most difficult of all techniques to master. Basic ikkyo is performed by the "defender" (nage) when their partner (uke) executes an overhead strike to nage's head. This strike is known as a *shomen* strike, or *shomen uchi*, and looks somewhat like uke dropping their hand down on nage's head like an axe. As uke strikes, nage reaches up with both hands and, making contact with uke's striking arm, directs uke's strike away from his head, turning uke's body off to one side and ultimately ending up with uke on the ground, his or her striking arm pinned to the mat.

I was about three years into my aikido training at the time, and while I had always struggled with that particular technique, all of the extra practice during the past three weeks had helped me get a better understanding and feel for it. As a result, and for the first time since I began my training, I felt as though I might just be finally starting to get a grip on how to perform ikkyo smoothly and effectively.

It was also during those three years that everyone in the class, myself included, had gotten into the habit of facing certain directions as uke and nage when training. For instance, the person acting as nage would always seem to end up facing the back of the dojo while the person acting as uke always faced the front. Uke would strike, nage would perform the technique; and when the technique was finished, both parties would stand up, go back to their respective positions, and begin again, with nage still facing the back of the dojo and uke facing the front.

As I said, I was feeling pretty good about how my technique seemed to be progressing, what with all of the extra practice we'd been putting in. But that night, something quite interesting happened that changed my perspective (both literally and figuratively) not only on my understanding of aikido but also on my understanding of certain aspects of horsemanship.

In the early stages of the evening, I had been the person performing the technique while my partner, who had been training about the same length of time as I had, was providing me with the strike I needed to do so. We had done several rounds of technique, always beginning with me, as nage, facing the rear of the dojo, my partner facing the front. However, after one such time of doing the technique, almost as an afterthought, I stood and faced my partner right there where I was, which was facing the far end of the dojo instead of returning to my customary position facing the back of the dojo. My partner stood and faced me, then struck. Much to my surprise, I suddenly found myself muddling haplessly through the technique that just a few seconds ago felt relatively smooth and effortless.

We tried again, and again; I just couldn't seem to get my rhythm down. On the third try, and after feeling a little out of sorts trying to work from the now unfamiliar position I had put myself in, I moved back to my original position, facing the back of the dojo with my partner facing the front. This time, the technique once again came through smoothly and easily.

By this time it was my partner's turn to act as nage and my turn to act as uke. As we got ready to switch roles, I noticed that, out of habit, we both also switched positions. He was then facing the back of the dojo and I was facing the front. We did the technique several times with everything going rather smoothly when I decided, more as an experiment than anything else, to reposition myself before striking. This time, instead of facing the front of the dojo, as I had been doing, I turned and faced the wall to my right, which caused him to face the opposite wall.

It was then that something very interesting happened. As I threw the strike toward my partner's head, he not only struggled with making contact with my arm, but he also had quite a bit of trouble performing the technique! We tried two more times from the same position, and both times he struggled with getting his technique to work properly, just as I had. For his last two attempts, we put ourselves back in our original positions, him facing the back wall and me facing the front, and just like that his technique came back.

All we had done was change the orientation of our bodies in relationship to where we were used to standing in the dojo when performing our techniques, and both of us were suddenly out of sync, not only with each other, but also with ourselves as individuals. Now I can't speak for my partner, but as for me, I realized that when my orientation changed that night, I had to fight the urge to get back to the original position, the position in which I was facing the back wall and he was facing the front.

That night after class, I gave the situation a great deal of thought and ultimately came to the conclusion that this problem with orientation during my aikido training was not at all a good thing. As a result, from that night forward, I began making a point to reorient myself whenever possible both while working on technique as well as when working on my strikes and grabs while performing the role of uke. I did find that at first, reorienting myself in the dojo was difficult and did cause me some problems. But as time went on, things did become much easier and smoother overall, and I found it interesting how much more comfortable I began to feel, regardless of the technique we were working on or the physical orientation of my body in relationship to where I was in the room.

But then, in addition to paying attention to how a change in orientation affected my techniques, I also began to look for and notice other things I was doing in the dojo in which I seemed dependent on a certain orientation in order to perform them well. One of these was my kata. Kata is a Japanese word that literally means "form," and a form is simply a series of detailed movements that we in our dojo practice individually and also as a group. These movements include stepping and turning along with various hand and arm movements all done with focus, precision, and intent. I realized that we, as a class, always practiced our kata facing the front of the dojo. But one evening after class, I took a few minutes and tried to perform the kata facing the back of the dojo, only to find even that wasn't as easy as I thought it would or should be.

Seeing how much of a problem the simple act of changing orientation was for me in the dojo, I began to wonder if this orientation anomaly might also be something that could affect horses as well.

———————

There were several times over the years while working various ranches that I witnessed something with horses that, even at the time, I found extremely interesting. This particular phenomenon (for lack of a better word) actually occurred on more than one occasion, with more than one horse. What I had noticed was that from time to time, when a new horse was brought to the ranch and turned into a pen or pasture for the first time, the horse (or horses) would go to a fence in the enclosure facing the direction from which it had last been before coming to the ranch.

For instance, I once bought a pair of draft horses from a place up in Minnesota, and after getting them home to the ranch, both horses walked right up to the fence in their pen and, as if drawn by a magnet, stood facing northeast—which would have eventually gotten them back to Minnesota if they were to walk a straight line back in that direction. In another instance, I had brought a horse from Denver in for training, and when turned into his pen, he stood facing southeast—again, the direction from which he had just come. Another horse from California stood facing west when he first arrived, and a mare from New Mexico stood facing south.

Still in another case, each summer for nine years we would bring our horses from our home in Estes Park to our friend's place near Loveland, Colorado, some thirty-five miles to the east and down a long winding canyon. These were the horses we would ultimately be using for the weeklong clinics we held there during the summer months. Once at our friend's place, the horses always stayed together in a pen near the driveway entrance, and every year, upon first arriving, one of our horses, a little dun gelding named Tuff, would walk to the northwest corner of the pen and stand staring back to the west, in the direction of home.

Even at the clinics we currently hold all over the world, whenever I see a horse that has been brought to a clinic by a participant, and the horse is worried and looking consistently in a certain direction, I have made a point to ask the riders where they were from. In the majority of those cases, I have found the worried horse is almost always looking toward the direction of home.

Now I certainly understand that what I have been witnessing over the years with these horses may be nothing more or less than simple coincidence. In fact, I'm not sure I would even argue the point if someone were to push me on it. However, I do know that it is not uncommon for animals of any kind to orient themselves back to a place where they have been comfortable in the past. We've all heard the stories of dogs or cats that have gotten lost hundreds and even thousands of miles from home only to somehow find their way back completely without help from humans.

On the other side of the coin, I'm sure we can all relate to that terrible sinking feeling that one gets when they they're lost, or even think they are lost. No doubt it would be a very similar feeling to what a horse might go through after having been uprooted and taken to a new or unfamiliar place. And it was this feeling of uncertainty and disorientation that I wanted folks to experience as part of our Aikido for Horsemen workshops.

During the workshop, we teach all of our students two separate katas designed specifically for horse people. The first kata, intended for new workshop students, has a series of very specific movements, which simulate getting in the saddle from the left side of the horse. Then the kata goes directly into the simulation of picking up a right lead, a turn on the haunches to the left, a left lead, a roll back to the right, another right lead, turn on the haunches to the left, left lead, then dismounting from the right. This kata is taught in pieces over a three-day period and is always practiced facing the front of the dojo.

On the last day, when all of the students have a good feel and ability to perform all of the separate movements in one flowing motion, we ask them to turn to their left then perform the kata facing the side of the dojo instead of the front of the dojo. In doing so, most students unconsciously try to reorient themselves back to doing the kata toward the front of the dojo, and some find they aren't able to complete the kata at all. Very few are able to actually complete the kata facing the new direction.

Once the students practice in the new direction and begin to get comfortable, we change the direction once more, and again, most are unable to complete the kata. It is then that we take the time to discuss the importance of orientation and how it affects our ability, or a horse's ability, to be comfortable. Many of the students, on their own, begin to make the connection between a horse that we might perceive as being "barn sour" and the fact that they may simply be disoriented in one way, shape, or form.

───────

When looking at the Thoroughbred gelding with the "barn sour" issue that we spoke about earlier from more of an *orientation* perspective than a behavioral perspective, things began to make a little more sense. For instance, I remember when the woman who owned the horse originally told me about what he was doing and how he was doing it. There was something she said in passing that, at the time, didn't really make much sense to me but had always stuck with me nonetheless. She told me that the horse would bolt back to the barn when she tried to ride him away from it, but he wouldn't try to get *in* the barn once back. Instead, he would run or pace circles in the area in front of the barn, then stop outside the front door, and almost always turn back toward the trail.

As I said, this was something that didn't make much sense to me at the time. After all, why would a horse go to all the trouble and energy of trying to get rid of a rider then run all the way back to where it wanted to be, only to stop short of its goal, which would seem to have been to get back *in* the barn? Unless, of course, getting *in* the barn wasn't the goal in the first place. And after having seen the gelding at our place and having listened to his owner before I began working with him, I began to wonder if the gelding's goal wasn't really to get back to the barn at all, but rather to simply get reoriented into a position where he felt comfortable.

What I mean by that is I remember his owner telling me that she couldn't understand why the gelding was so barn sour in the first place, as she didn't think he liked living in the barn anyway. She said he always seemed cranky in his stall and had often taken to pacing and weaving if he were left in it for long periods of time. In fact, he would usually be in a rush to get out of his stall and only settled down once outside. She also mentioned that she didn't understand why the horse would always run back to the front of the barn as she had never taken the horse in the barn through the front door, but rather she always took him in the barn through the side or back doors, as those were usually closer to his daily turn out areas.

However, she did always take the gelding *out* the front door. And it was this piece of information, along with my new understanding of the importance of orientation, that finally got me to think that maybe what the horse was doing with his unwanted actions was trying to get himself back to a position where he was *visually* triggered into feeling better. If he was stressed and uncomfortable the entire time he was in his stall, then the first opportunity he would have to feel better may have been when he stepped outside. This would have been when he came out the front door, and thus he would have no doubt associated feeling better with the *visual* orientation of looking outward from the front of the barn, not getting back inside.

If this were the case, then him wanting to get back to the barn never really was his main focus. Getting himself into a position where he could stand and look away from it would have been his primary goal, and in order for him to do that, he would first need to get back to the barn. Still, it was the way the gelding would try to get back to the barn that caused most horse folks (including me at the time) to assume they were dealing with a "barn sour" issue.

The gelding wanting to get to the front of a barn so he could look away from it would also explain why he would have wanted to get back to our barn when I had taken him out on the trail that first time. He would have wanted to try to feel better the only way he knew how, and if that was getting in front of a building and looking away from it, he would have headed for the first one he saw. So even though he had never been in or really even been around our barn before, that wouldn't have mattered. What would have mattered was him getting himself into a physical position in relation to the building that would have triggered him into a calmer state of mind.

This would also explain why he had so much trouble calming himself down when put in the various pastures near the barn and close to other horses. Being able to see the barn wouldn't have helped him, and neither would the presence of other horses. In fact, even putting him *in* the barn wouldn't have helped. The only thing that probably would have helped was for him to be *close* to the barn so he could orient himself away from it.

I think this idea of orientation also crosses over in many ways to a horse appearing to be what we might refer to as buddy sour or herd bound. You see, on top of horses being extremely social animals, they also seem to have an innate ability to become very attached to another horse or group of horses they come in contact with when they find themselves in a strange or unfamiliar situation. Many people are amazed at the speed at which this apparent connection between horses can be made, even when the contact between the horses is very brief or even just in passing.

For instance, I'm sure most trail riders at one time or another have experienced how a horse they were riding suddenly seemed to become attached to a strange horse that passed them on the trail, or witnessed how a horse might become anxious, nervous, or concerned when seeing another horse or horses off in the distance. I also think that many horse folks may have heard of or experienced the way that two horses that have never met before can be put in a trailer for a ride to some nearby destination and come out just a short time later acting as if they've been married to each other for twenty years.

On numerous occasions at our clinics, we've seen something very similar happen between participant horses that were complete strangers upon arriving at the venue. These horses, when stalled next to each other for even less than twenty-four hours, often become so bonded that when one is brought to the arena to be worked, both it and its neighbor end up spending much of that time calling back and forth to each other.

I mentioned earlier how horses are not very well equipped to handle being suddenly put into strange or unexpected situations. In nature, it is not something that they do. Yet we put domestic horses in strange and unexpected situations all the time—whether we are taking them on a trail ride in an area they've never been in before, taking them to a show or clinic, or simply just changing boarding facilities.

Every time we do these things with a horse, they can end up disoriented to one degree or another and thus often end up under some kind of stress. Once under that stress, they will do whatever they can to find a way to feel better. Sometimes that will mean latching on to another horse—even one they've never met before. Sometimes that will mean trying to orient themselves back in the direction of home, and sometimes, like with the Thoroughbred gelding, they try to find something that is visually familiar to them.

Of course, us humans usually don't give this kind of thing a second thought because the vast majority of us have been going to strange and unfamiliar places since we were very young. As a result, the act of doing so is no longer stressful to us. For us, traveling to new places has become part of life. For most of us, traveling began when we were kids with something as simple as our parents putting us in the car and taking us to grandma's house clear across town. Or perhaps we were taken to the movie theater or grocery store or any number of other places that might have seemed strange to us at first. Still, over time, and the more we did it, traveling to new and different places simply became as ordinary as climbing out of bed in the morning.

Another thing about us humans is even when we were kids and being taken somewhere by our parents, we generally knew what the destination was. Seldom would our parents take us somewhere without first telling us where we were going. As a result, our destination was seldom a surprise. When a horse gets into a trailer, on the other hand, the destination is almost always a surprise. I've often thought that a trailer ride for a horse must be similar to us taking a ride in a time machine. They climb in a box, it rattles around for a while, they get out, and they're someplace completely different. Not only that, but they had no control over where they went or how they got there. I've often wondered if maybe this might be the reason some horses refuse to get in trailers to begin with. The disorientation they experience at the end of the journey may simply be too much for them.

Still, other horses do very well traveling to new and unfamiliar places, being in shows, or getting out on trail rides, and I believe there are three main reasons for this. First, many of these horses are extremely familiar with their job—whatever that job might happen to be. Second, they trust their owners and/or riders, and third, they have gotten familiar with and had the opportunity to practice the art of orientation.

I believe horses that know what their job is and how to perform it well have much less trouble adjusting to new places than one that doesn't know their job well. My guess is a horse that understands how to perform its job would be a lot like a human that understood theirs. A human who is highly skilled and experienced in a certain trade could easily travel from one employer to another, and although the location of the job might be different, the one constant would be the job itself. As a result, the human is able to perform the work in the new environment with relative ease.

Horses appear to be able to do the same thing. Skilled and experienced ranch horses travel to new environments all the time, and most make the transition from one place to another with very little trouble at all. Skilled and experienced trail horses do the same thing, as do show horses. Now, one might notice here that I made a point to say that it's the skilled *and* experienced horses that don't seem to have the trouble. The horses that I'm talking about seem to have to be both. Just having one or the other doesn't always appear to be good enough.

There are a lot of skilled show horses out there—horses that have been taught the mechanics of showing, usually in a safe home environment—that completely fall apart in the show ring due to the fact that they don't have much *experience* actually traveling to new places and performing. By the same token, I've worked with a lot of very experienced trail horses—horses who have spent years doing nothing but trail rides—who are lacking in the actual *skills* they need to be good trail horses. These skills might include knowing how to stop, turn, back up, and transition well. As a result, many of these horses, even though they have spent countless hours on the trails, never seem to be able to settle down completely when taken to new places, or they may bolt when something unexpected happens, or they may also be the ones that want to attach themselves to any strange horse they pass or come in contact with.

Now having said all that, I also believe that there is one variable that can make up for either a horse's lack of skill or lack of experience, and that is the horse's trust in its rider/handler. Horses are born followers, and it has been my experience that if the horse's rider has proven him or herself to be a good leader to the horse through their consistent handling, behavior, and prudent decision making, even a horse with low confidence or limited skills will be more likely to willingly go with them and/or follow them into most strange or unfamiliar situations or places.

It has also been my experience that when these qualities are present, that is, the horse having both skill and experience in the job we are asking of them, and when they have trust and confidence in their rider/handler, it then seems much easier for them to settle in to a new place or situation. Again, much like most humans when we go to a new place or situation, these horses seem to find a way to orient or familiarize themselves to the new surroundings fairly easily and relatively quickly.

Over the years I have watched as the horses we travel with get out of the trailer at a venue that is sometimes thousands of miles from home and, when placed in a pen or pasture, immediately familiarize themselves with the fence lines, water supply, and feed area. They then make themselves at home and settle down to the task of eating and sleeping. When it's time to go to work, they go out and get the job done as if they were still in the comfortable surroundings of our place back home.

I'm fairly certain that at least part of the reason they adjust so quickly to new environments is because they are extremely experienced at traveling. However, I also think it may be because we are with them pretty much twenty-four hours a day. In terms of orientation, and because we are really the only thing that is constant in their lives while on the road, it isn't such a far stretch to assume that they may see us as at least one potential and generalized point of reference when coming into a new situation. As a result, rather than orienting themselves to a specific direction (for instance) in order to feel comfortable, they end up putting at least some of their trust, and therefore comfort, in us.

I should also point out here that that trust and comfort go both ways. As anyone who has spent any time at all in the company of a trustworthy horse a long way from home can attest, there is an awful lot to be said for being able to put your faith and confidence on the stability of a highly dependable mount.

—————

I realize that there probably aren't a lot of people out there that have the opportunity to spend the kind of time with their horses that we do and, as such, may be dealing with some of the issues I mentioned, such as a horse being barn sour, buddy sour, or herd bound. And I guess that's the bad news. However, there is also good news. And that good news is that horses, like people, have the ability to change the way they feel about how they see and how they feel when in new and unfamiliar places and situations.

Early on, I spoke about the problems I had with both my technique as well as my kata when the orientation of my body in relationship to the inside of the dojo had changed. When this first happened, I found I was extremely uncomfortable and had a hard time getting my body to perform those tasks and techniques that I thought (after years of practice) I knew so well.

Well, the truth is, I did know the tasks and techniques. That wasn't the issue. The problem, it turns out, was that while I had gone through the motions of learning and practicing everything I had been taught, I had only taken the information in on a mechanical level. All of the information was just on the outside of me, and very little of it had gone all the way to the inside. In other words, what I *hadn't* done was internalize the information and make it a component of who I was as an individual.

What I have come to realize is the internalization of the information is the glue that holds everything together. For that reason, when I found my technique was only practiced on a mechanical level, it became much more difficult for the information and mechanics to work together in concert. So when the surroundings changed, so did my mechanics. I had found that when the mechanics seemingly change without our control, both frustration and worry set in and anxiety begins to rise. Once that happens, we try, sometimes unconsciously, to reorient ourselves back into a position where we are comfortable so our mechanics can take over again.

Yet, when the mechanics and information become part of us, it is then much easier to find comfort and stability from within rather than having to rely on a specific physical orientation from which to draw comfort. I believe this may be the kind of thing that happens with our horses, too, particularly in the case of horses that appear buddy sour, barn sour, or herd bound.

The Thoroughbred gelding I spoke about earlier, for instance, had gotten so locked into relying on gaining comfort from a very specific orientation in relation to a building that the only way he thought he could feel better when stressed was to get himself back in that, or a similar physical position. Yet when he was placed in a situation in which he was allowed to work through his stress and anxiety that didn't actually include that particular orientation, the orientation no longer became a necessary part of the process. As a result, he found he could find confidence and comfort from within instead of having to rely on some arbitrary outside source to attain reassurance.

This is exactly the same thing that happened to me during my process in the dojo, after I found the quality of my technique was becoming directly tied to the position of my body in relation to the inside of the room. While it was initially a struggle and while I sometimes found it difficult to make adjustments when trying to reorient myself, the end result was that I became way more comfortable overall and ultimately found I no longer needed that certain orientation to execute my techniques properly. This also allowed me to ultimately be able to travel to different dojos across the country and train with different people and in different styles of aikido and still operate with confidence and at a relatively competent level.

This appears to be the same thing that happens with horses that work through their apparent issues with orientation. Once they have gotten through the initial shock of not being able to calm themselves in the way they had come to rely on, they almost immediately begin to search for another way to feel better. It has been my experience that when set up properly and given enough time, most will not only find they don't really need their former "safety blanket," but their confidence level jumps quickly and dramatically.

It is then that they begin to find comfort and stability from within, and along with no longer needing their outside source of comfort, they also find the things that used to bother them no longer do. Horses like the Thoroughbred gelding who couldn't seem to get more than a few feet from the barn without wanting to get back using any means necessary ultimately end up being able to confidently go out on trails with their rider regardless of the familiarity of the trail or the distance traveled.

Every technique in aikido has one common thread. That is that at some point during each technique, both uke and nage will end up, even if just for a second, facing the same direction. The reason for this is that it gives nage a clear view of what his attacker's perspective was prior to attacking. In other words, nage is trying to physically see things from his attacker's point of view.

I really appreciate this aspect of aikido for a variety of reasons, not the least of which is that it both figuratively and literally allows us to see things from another perspective. But perhaps even more important (at least for me) is that the concept doesn't really allow for stagnation in our own point of view. In other words, it gives the opportunity to change our orientation in a way that, if we let it, will help us take in the big picture—a 360-degree view of the time and space that surrounds us at that given moment.

I believe it is this same type of ultimate understanding and acceptance of one's environment that allows both horses and people to become comfortable within themselves, which in turn allows them to rely less on a certain orientation within that environment and more on acceptance of the situation as a whole.

Since I began taking a really good look at this idea of orientation in relation to how it affects both horses and humans, I've come to understand it comes in many shapes and forms, and it can work for us just as easily as it can work against us. Not only that, but the more I look at and pay attention to situations that involve certain behavioral issues with horses, the more it appears those issues can be traced back to either a problem with orientation or a problem with disorientation.

Now of course I am certainly not trying to claim that this is the cause and solution to *all* training issues that horses develop, but I do believe it is the cause and solution to some, primarily the ones we've already discussed. All that being said, I must say I sure am looking forward to seeing what other applications might arise from just taking a little closer look at this idea of orientation in the years to come.

Chapter 8
Movement and Openings

───────────

"So you want me to just turn her loose?" the woman asked.

"Yup," I said, opening the gate to the arena. "Take her in and turn her loose."

"What if she tries to jump the fence?"

"Has she ever tried to jump a fence before?"

"No."

"Then she probably won't now." I shrugged as the woman brought the big bay mare into the arena, and I closed the gate behind them.

I could completely understand the woman's concern and worry that her horse might try to escape the arena once turned loose, especially after what had transpired earlier that day. The mare, a Dutch Warmblood, had come to the clinic so that her owner and she could work on their transitions. However, their session hadn't gone quite as planned. The mare had lived most of her life as a dressage horse and had spent the majority of that time in the confines of one relatively quiet arena or another. On this day, she nearly lost her mind when she saw the small herd of roping cattle that lived in a holding pen just outside the far end of the arena that we were working in.

Pretty much our entire session had been spent in the farthest corner of the arena from the cattle, right next to the gate, trying to get the mare to quiet down enough to ride, which we were eventually able to do but not until most of the time for the rider's session had passed. This mare had never seen cattle before, and she was pretty convinced they were there for the express purpose of killing her. As a result, she had become so focused on staying alive that learning anything while being ridden, or even just being ridden in the first place, hadn't even been on her radar screen.

The rider was considering pulling the mare from the clinic due to her apparent overwhelming fear of the nearby cattle, and the fact that in order to get anything done, she would need to ride in relative proximity to them. From all outward indications, that didn't appear to be likely, and because there was no place else for the cattle to go, it also didn't seem likely to the owner that the pair would be getting anything worthwhile done while they were there.

The truth is, I couldn't have agreed with her more. There was no question we weren't going to be able to get much done with the pair if things stayed as they were. In fact, the mare had left the arena at the end of their session in only a slightly better frame of mind than when she came in. Still, the last thing I wanted to do was have the woman take the horse home without at least trying to see if we could help her feel better about the situation in general, and perhaps even the cattle specifically.

Because of that, I had asked the woman following her session if she would be willing to bring the mare back to the arena at the end of the day. I wanted to try to set something up for the mare to see if we might be able to help her overcome her fear of the cattle without us having to do much in the way of "training," and her not having to do much in the way of fretting. The woman agreed.

After I had finished with the last rider of the day, the woman brought her mare back to the arena. The closer the mare got, the more anxious she began to get until by the time she got to the gate, her head was so high she looked a little like a giraffe, and she was blowing such loud warning snorts they could be heard echoing off the neighbor's buildings over a quarter mile away.

"Go ahead and take her in," I had said. "Then just turn her loose."

I had explained that even as scared as the mare appeared, I felt that if we gave her a little time alone in the pen to sort things out on her own that she probably would. The owner was skeptical, and rightly so, especially after how badly the mare had felt about the situation earlier in the day. Still, she was willing to give it a try, and so she took the mare in the pen and turned her loose, albeit rather reluctantly.

As soon as she was turned loose, the mare snorted, turned, and ran for the area where we had been working earlier in the day. She frantically paced back and forth using only about thirty feet of the ninety-foot fence, staring over the fence toward the stall she had been kept in during the day and calling loudly to no one in particular. This went on for about five minutes before I grabbed a few buckets and a couple traffic cones that were lying nearby and placed them directly on the path she was using to pace the fence. This caused her to have to turn her full attention from the direction of her stall to having at least some of it back in the arena and to where she was placing her feet when she moved along the fence line.

Doing this broke up the pattern she had been using to pace the fence, which basically had been six steps to the right, duck her head toward the fence, turn, five steps back to the left, duck her head toward the fence, turn, then back to the right again. She had repeated this pattern so many times in just the five minutes that she had been in the arena that her feet fell in the exact same hoof marks with each step she took, and she was digging small trenches in the areas where she was turning around.

The cones and buckets caused her to change her path just enough to where she began moving farther down the fence where there were no obstacles that she would have to think about while moving. Once out of the path of the obstacles, she began pacing once again, and once again, I placed obstacles in her way. This caused her to move again, and again I placed obstacles in her way. The obstacles were placed in such a haphazard pattern that she wasn't able to develop a rhythm to her stride. This in turn caused her to go from looking almost exclusively over the fence in the direction of her stall to looking almost exclusively at the ground in front of her feet.

By this time she was walking the entire fence line, trying her best to weave her way through the cones, buckets, and now tires and ground poles that I had placed there in an attempt to find some sort of pattern in the mess. It was difficult for her to do, but any time she was able to start to develop a pattern, I quickly shifted some of the obstacles around to block the pattern from developing.

The reason I didn't want her to develop a pattern in her movement was that it is very easy for horses to fall into some sort of pattern when they're under stress and then use the pattern to keep themselves from giving any thought to the situation. If they aren't thinking about the situation, they won't take the time to figure out a solution.

After nearly thirty minutes, the mare had gone from a frantic trot with her body tight, her head over the fence, and screaming loudly back in the direction of her stall to a relatively quiet walk with her head down and inside the pen most of the time. Still, she wouldn't look in the direction of the cattle. When she needed to turn, she continued to turn toward the fence, averting her eyes from the bothersome stimuli at the other end of the arena. But before long, even that changed.

I figured if she could find it in herself to turn and look at the cattle, eventually she was bound to work her way down to investigate them. But she would first need to look at them, and that was the thing that seemed near impossible for her to do. However, around forty minutes after placing her in the pen, she finally did. It was just a quick glimpse that she threw their way as she made what would be her very first turn to the inside of the arena after countless turns to the outside, but it was all that was needed.

The brief glimpse turned into a little longer glimpse on her next turn, and the turn after that, she actually stopped for just a second while she looked to the far end of the arena. As she went back to pacing the fence, I placed a cone, very near where she had stopped to look at the cattle, which caused her to take a little wider turn in that area. On the next turn she veered away from the fence, around the cone, and toward the cattle. This time she was noticeably closer to the cattle, even though it was only a few feet closer. She stopped for several seconds and then headed back to the debris-littered fence line she had been walking. A few turns after that, she turned from the fence, took fifteen or twenty steps in the direction of the cattle, raised her head, and let out one of her loud warning snorts.

One of the steers flung his head over his back to shoo a swarm of flies from between his shoulders, and the mare galloped back to the fence and resumed her pacing. This time she paced for only two laps before trotting away from the fence and toward the cattle to about the same spot as where she had stopped before. Again she raised her head and snorted, nodded her head up and down, then snorted again. Unfazed, the cattle rested lazily under the limbs of the young oak tree that grew in the middle of the pen.

She snorted again, took three wary steps in their direction, and then bolted back to the fence. She repeated this a number of times during the next fifteen minutes, each time getting just a little closer to the cattle than the last, and each time galloping just as fast as she could go back to the fence. By the time she had worked herself to the middle of the arena, she was lowering her head and looking inquisitively toward the cattle instead of looking at them in the near-panicked way she had been previously. By the time she was two-thirds across the arena, it appeared as though some sort of invisible magnetic force was pulling her toward them. She would walk a few feet then stop and lean backward, sometimes turning and bolting, only to immediately turn and trot back to where she had just been.

Nearly an hour and a half after we had originally placed the mare in the arena by herself, she had finally, ever so cautiously, made her way all the way to the pen the cattle were in. A few minutes after that, she was standing nose to nose with two of them, all three smelling each other and seemingly becoming best of friends.

The next morning when the mare's owner brought her in for their session, the woman mounted up, and the mare immediately took the woman right up to the pen the cattle were in. They stood there for a few minutes while the mare said hello to her newfound friends, then the pair came back, and we all went to work.

Following the session, the horse's owner told me that not only was her mare the calmest she had ever been during a training session, but she was also way more responsive than she had ever been as well. "Is that because of the way we worked with her today?" the woman asked. "Or because she wasn't afraid of the cattle?"

"I expect it's a little of both," I said. "But I'm sure her feeling more confident about her surroundings sure didn't hurt."

———

I have told this particular story a number of times over the years to people all over the world. I often use it as an example for riders who are trying to force their horse into situations that the horse might feel are frightening or even potentially life threatening, faster than the horse is willing or able to go. I do this because many people often overlook the fact that horses can't just throw away instinctual safety features that have been installed over millions of years of evolution simply because we're in a hurry to get something done.

I also like to tell this story because it illustrates a couple of key elements that many of us miss when it comes to working with a frightened horse. The first is obviously the amount of time a horse will take to familiarize themselves with something they aren't sure of compared to how fast we think they should familiarize themselves with it. And the second is the way in which they do it.

Most horse folks will try to march a horse right up to something that is frightening to him or her, and then expect the horse to stand there stock still while he or she figures out what the scary thing is, and at the same time somehow magically and completely loses his or her fear of the thing. However, when we look at all the movement the Warmblood mare used to help herself feel better, there is a pretty stark contrast between the two.

In fact, I dare say there are very few riders out there that, when trying to help a frightened horse feel better about something that was scaring them, would allow the horse to gallop wildly away from the scary thing. Yet, not only was that exactly what the mare did when left to her own designs, but it also seemed to play a major role in the success of the process she went through to get over her fear. It might be important to note here that the reason running was so beneficial to the mare in the first place is because movement in horses, as well as in people, is one of the keys to releasing nervous energy stored in the body.

However, when humans are on horses and something scary happens, whether it frightens the horse or the rider, one of the single most common reactions in the human is to try and get the horse to stop moving. Unfortunately, this usually only causes things to escalate (as most horses don't like being told to stand still when their instincts tell them to move) and then very often what would have only been a minor issue between horse and rider often ends up being a major problem.

A training technique that has really taken hold over the last twenty or so years, and that I believe is a major contributor to this miscommunication between horse and rider, is a practice most people would refer to as a "one rein" stop. During the one rein stop, the rider intentionally brings the horse's head around laterally until the horse's nose almost (and in some cases actually does) touches the rider's boot. Basically, what this does is cause the horse to disengage its hindquarters, or move its hindquarters in the opposite direction the head is facing, which in turn takes the horse's power away and ultimately causes him or her to stop their feet.

Now admittedly, this is a very effective way to get most horses to stop during a potentially dangerous situation or in a situation in which the horse is out of control or getting ready to be out of control. However, what the one-rein stop doesn't do is allow the horse to expend energy, which is usually what the horse is trying to do in the first place. It is for that reason that many horses that have been pulled into a one-rein stop will feel just as scared, jittery, or explosive *after* they've been stopped as they had *before* they were stopped—some even more.

I look at a horse's energy and movement a lot like water in the banks of a stream or river. As long as the water is moving within the banks, everything is usually pretty all right. However, if we build a dam in the river—and not a very good dam at that—it doesn't stop the river from flowing. It only builds up the energy of the river behind the dam, magnifying its power. Eventually, because the dam wasn't a good one to start with, the dam breaks, and now there not only is a big mess upstream where the water had backed up and flooded the area, but there is also a big mess downstream where it is flooded as well.

For me, this is what the one-rein stop often does with a horse's energy. The stop itself doesn't prevent the energy from flowing; it just allows for the buildup of energy behind the stop. So when the horse is finally allowed to go straight again, they become a lot like the floodwater that was built up behind the now-broken dam.

Putting it another way, the one-rein stop is often used less for teaching a horse what the proper response in a stressful situation might be and more to temporarily take away their power. The end result is a relatively common theme in most horse training circles—we end up telling the horse what we *don't* want, but not explaining to them what we *do* want.

———————

Many years ago I was asked to work with a horse that had trouble walking when he was taken out on the trail. That isn't to say he didn't go out on the trail, because he did, and it isn't to say that he was worried or upset when on the trail, because he wasn't. He just always went a lot faster on the trail than his owner, who had owned him less than six months, wanted him to go. The main reason the horse, a big paint gelding, had so much trouble trying to slow down on the trail was that going fast is what his previous owner had taught him to do. Whenever his old owner trail rode him, he always did so either at a trot or a lope, almost never walk, and most certainly never a slow walk. As a result, the gelding simply associated being on the trail with going fast, so that's what he did.

The new owner, a woman named Becky and a fair hand with a horse in her own right, had already spent quite a bit of time with the gelding trying to get him to slow down, and nothing she had done had achieved the results she was looking for. In fact, the first time I went to her place and watched her ride him, I quite honestly didn't know if there was anything I was going to be able to do for him either. He seemed pretty set in his ways and not terribly interested in changing what he did and how he did it. Still, Becky had hired me to ride him, and it was good weather that day, so I figured if nothing else, I'd ride him around for a while and see if some stroke of genius would come over me.

He left the barn just fine, with no hint of worry or wanting to go fast, and nothing changed in his demeanor as we crossed the gravel road in front of Becky's place. However, literally no sooner had he set foot on the dirt path that led up the bank of the irrigation ditch we would be riding on than his high gear suddenly kicked in. He had been so quiet up to that point that his burst of energy took me by surprise, and I was almost unseated as he bolted forward and shot up the bank.

This was back in the days where more times than not, when I rode a horse like this, I would let them run until they couldn't run anymore and then keep working them until I felt they had given up the idea of running altogether unless they were asked to do so. The problem was, Becky had already tried that. Not once, not twice, but a number of times, and if anything, the gelding simply got stronger and faster each time she did it. She had also done her version of a one-rein stop with him every time he tried to run or trot off down the trail, and again, every time she would let him out of the stop, he would just go right back to what he was doing before she had stopped him. She had also tried a number of other techniques, all of which I would have used, and none had worked. So as the two of us shot up the bank, I must say I was a little at a loss as to what to do with him next.

Still, whatever I was going to do I would need to do it pretty quickly because within seconds of crossing the road, we were already up the bank and on our way down the trail. We weren't out of control, mind you, just going fast . . . real fast. We covered a couple hundred yards in no time at all, and I'm pretty sure we were passing things along the side of the bank, I just couldn't make any of them out as they were all moving by at a blur.

After those two or three hundred yards, I decided we had gone far enough and fast enough, and more as a way to slow things down than anything else, I just turned the gelding in a relatively tight circle. Now the top of the bank was large enough to drive a truck on, some twelve or fifteen feet wide, and it offered plenty of room for us to circle without running the risk of falling off the bank on to the road below or coming off into the water on the other side.

I was not only surprised at the speed the gelding was able to travel in the tight little circle I'd put him in, but I was also equally surprised at how easy it seemed for him to maintain that speed. We circled at least twenty times right there on the spot, his head turned to the inside of the circle without any break in speed whatsoever, so in an attempt to break things up a little, I turned him quickly and put him in a circle in the opposite direction. He flipped directions easily but did have to slow down ever so slightly to do so. I let him circle in the new direction for several laps before flipping him back to the original direction. Again, he needed to slow slightly to change directions. It was really the only time since we had gotten on the bank that he'd even thought about going slower, so I quickly decided if

I was going to help him slow down at all, changing directions on the circle might be my way in.

I flipped him again and, after just a couple laps, flipped him back. Less than a lap later, I flipped him the other direction, ran one lap after that and then we went the other way again. I continued to turn him one way then the other and then back for the better part of fifteen or twenty minutes before seemingly out of nowhere, he offered to walk. At that point, I immediately stopped turning him and let him go straight. Much to my and the horse's surprise, we found he was, indeed, able to slowly walk while on the trail. Unfortunately, he was only able to walk a few steps before he once again broke back into a trot, and as soon as I felt the trot building, I began asking him to circle again.

We reversed directions several more times before he offered to walk, and when he did, I let him go straight. After walking about five or six steps, he began speeding up, and as he did, I circled him. We continued working in this way for the better part of an hour and a half, building on the steps he could put together in the walk, and circling the steps that were faster than that. Within what I would consider a relatively short period of time, the gelding had figured out that while going fast wasn't necessarily a bad thing, traveling at an easy walk was what I was really looking for. As a result, by the time we returned from our trail ride, the gelding had not only learned how to slow down, but he actually seemed to enjoy walking quietly instead of stampeding off.

I suppose at first glance, these two stories that I related—the one about the big mare afraid of cattle and this one about the gelding that had trouble finding a way to slow himself down on the trail—may seem unrelated. After all, one horse seemed to be extremely troubled by a scary "outside" source and ultimately was able to work through her issue on her own while the other horse's problem was man-made, and as such, he needed considerable help and guidance from a rider to work through his. Yet, when we look a little closer, both are actually very similar in a number of ways.

The first, and perhaps most obvious similarity between the two horses, is that movement played a major role in helping them both resolve their respective issues. It could be argued that the mare self-regulated her speed and movement while the gelding needed help and guidance regulating his speed and movement. However, the fact remains that both relied on movement, and regulation of that movement, to bring their respective issues to a conclusion.

Be that as it may, the one similarity between the two that I find even more important is something that can, and very often is, easily overlooked when working with horses. Put simply, in both cases it was the very brief gaps, or breaks, in each horse's seemingly set behavior that ultimately allowed for redirection of thought and energy. I refer to these gaps in behavior as *openings* and, whenever present, can become a very powerful tool to help direct even a worried or distracted horse toward a more positive goal.

Now before going any further, I should probably point out that I see an *opening* as anything that allows us to help guide, however briefly, an individual in the direction we ultimately would like them to go. An opening can be, and often is, a very subtle form of communication between horse and rider that can easily slip past us if we're not paying attention. In the case of these two horses, the openings were indeed pretty subtle.

The mare's opening came as she paced the fence. After reversing herself time and time again toward the fence while she paced, for whatever reason she suddenly decided to turn away from it and toward the cattle. Once that little opening presented itself, I quickly set a up a cone very near to where she had turned so in the event she turned in the same spot again, the cone would cause her to swing a little wider, which would in turn give her a longer look at the cattle. I believe her being able to stop and look at the cattle, as she was able to do on the next pass, was at least part of the incentive leading up to her eventually trying to work her way over to them.

In the case of the gelding, the openings he presented and used actually worked both for and against what we were trying to do with him. The part that worked for us happened as I was turning him. When doing so, he would usually go very easily into the turn. However, after several laps, I could feel him beginning to offer to go the other direction. This came as he began to lean in the opposite direction of the current turn. In other words, when turning to the right, for instance, I would be using the right rein to ask for the turn, and he would put up very little if any resistance. After a few laps, I would start feeling resistance in the rein, a sign he perhaps wanted to go back to the left. At that point, I would flip him to the left. When I began feeling resistance to the right, I would turn him to the right. As a result, it was in this resistance that the opening for redirection presented itself.

At that point of resistance, turning was easy because that was the direction he wanted to go anyway. It also ended up taking his energy away, as much of his energy was built upon resistance in the first place. What I mean by that is whenever he would go fast on the trail, riders would always pull on the reins in one way, shape, or form in order to try and slow him. This pulling gave the gelding something to lean against and actually increased his power, which helped him go faster. So the thing people were using in order to try to slow him down actually tightened his body and helped increase his speed. However, without anything to push against, his power began to dissipate, his body began to soften, and eventually he was able to slow himself for brief periods. It was this slowing that we were then able to ultimately build upon in order to help him get to a walk.

Of course on the other side of the coin was the opening the gelding was able to find and which he was able to use to help speed himself back up. That would happen once he had slowed to a walk and I let him out of the circle with slack in the reins. He would quietly walk a few steps in that straight line, and with the slack now present, he saw that as an opening, and off he'd go again.

But I believe the thing that helped negate him continuing to see slack in the reins as an invitation to speed up was the fact that as soon as his energy began building, I would do my best to quickly turn him back into the circle, at which time the entire process would start over. Sometimes I wasn't able to catch him until after he'd already taken a few steps at the faster speed, and other times, I was able to catch him just as the thought to speed up began to cross his mind. That thought usually manifested itself as an overall tightening of his body just before he wanted to take off.

The point I guess I'm trying to make here is that openings can and do work both ways. When we look for or are aware of any openings horses present that might allow us to help direct them toward our ultimate goal, training can actually become relatively easy. However, much like a game of chess, while we are looking for openings to help direct the horse, the horse may also be looking for openings that will allow him or her to continue in the direction they are already comfortable with or in the direction they believe to be true and correct—whether that direction is actually beneficial for them or not.

———————

Something else that might be worth mentioning here is that in general, openings are much easier to find or create when movement is present. One of my aikido instructors has a saying he likes to use when it comes to this idea, which is "A body in motion stays in motion, a body stopped has a tendency to stay stopped." Perhaps another way to say that might be that it is often easier to keep something moving than it is to get it moving. I think anybody who has ever had to deal with a horse that didn't want to go forward for whatever reason can certainly relate to that.

Still, it amazes me just how small an opening can actually be, whether working with horses or with people, and how easy it can be to create an opening when one is needed. One of my very first conscious realizations of the power of the proper use of an opening occurred during an aikido class I was in several years ago.

That particular night, our instructor had been talking quite a bit about openings and how we can use them to our advantage while performing our techniques. Up till that night, my idea and definition of an "opening" in relation to martial arts was limited to thinking of it in terms of a weakness in one's defenses. Sort of like a boxer who spends so much energy guarding his face that he ends up leaving his midsection vulnerable to attack. While that could certainly be considered one way of looking at it, on this night I was to learn a completely different definition of the word and of its use and, in the process, find a completely different way of looking at working with horses.

When the evening started, our instructor had discussed the type of opening he wanted us to look for, but somehow—probably because I already had a preconceived notion on the subject—I had missed the subtleties of what he was talking about. As we went through the evening doing a number of different techniques, I found I had been spending much of my time looking for what *my* definition of an "opening" was in my partner's technique which, as I said, was really nothing more or less than trying to spot a weakness that I could exploit.

About halfway through class, our instructor brought the training to a stop and, I'm sure not by coincidence, asked me to come to the front of the dojo to help him demonstrate the point he was trying to make regarding *his* version of openings. He explained that an "opening" can be created in an opponent long before making contact with them. But in order for that to happen, one first needs to be thinking less about fighting and more about offering direction.

I heard his words, but to be honest, I was more concerned about keeping myself as covered up and guarded as possible when he asked me to do whatever it was that he was going to ask me to do to demonstrate his point. He then asked that I give him a medium-speed punch to his midsection with my right hand, which I did. He easily stepped to the side as my punch reached him, and my fist brushed past him harmlessly.

"This is one way of dealing with this situation," he said, asking me to go back to my original position and get ready to punch again. "But by moving aside, while effective in certain situations, doesn't help us make a connection with our partner, and it is difficult to give him direction."

He returned to his original position and motioned for me to throw another punch, which I did. He once again moved out of the way, but this time he grabbed my wrist as it breezed past him. As he grabbed me, I immediately tightened my entire body in defense. "This is another way to handle the situation," our instructor said. "But you can see that by me grabbing him tightly, it causes my partner to stiffen and become defensive, also making it difficult for me to direct him."

We both returned to our original positions. He signaled for me to throw the punch, which I did. But this time, as I threw it and even before he made contact with me, I felt myself falling ever so slightly toward him as he moved to the side. The next thing I knew he had touched my arm, and then I was lying face-first on the mat with no idea how I got there. I quickly got to my feet and faced him, but he was already turned and talking to the rest of the students.

"Creating an opening can happen even before we make contact," he said, motioning me to get ready to punch again. "By *thinking* about where you want your partner to go, you are already creating that opening." He nodded for me to strike. Again, as my punch drew near him and before he made contact with my arm, I felt my body fading slightly in his direction. He touched my arm and down I went.

I quickly got to my feet and faced him, ready to throw another punch if I was instructed to do so. "*Think* about where you want him to go," he repeated. "By thinking about where you want him to go, *you* are already going there, which creates an invitation for him to go there as well." He nodded for me to strike.

For the third time in a row, I felt my body drifting as my punch got close to him. This time, however, I was drifting away from him, not toward him, and as he made contact with me, I felt myself spinning slightly away from him then being drawn back toward him, and then I dropped to the floor. I once again rose to my feet and faced him, ready to attack again if requested.

"This time," he said as he faced me, "go slow so people can see."

I threw the punch as if in slow motion and watched my instructor carefully as he stepped out of the way. I hadn't been able to tell what he had been doing that caused me to go to the mat so easily, so I had hoped this time maybe I could see it. Once out of the way of my punch, he asked that I freeze in place. With me then standing as if frozen in time, he stood next to me and asked that the other students watch my body. Within seconds, I felt myself ever so slightly being drawn toward him. "You see." He smiled. "Once your partner has found the opening you've provided—he reached up and touched my arm—directing them is easy." He gently moved his hand on my arm, and I helplessly crumpled to the mat.

He would go on to explain and then show how, in addition to simply thinking about the direction he wanted me to go, he had also set his body up in a way that allowed me to do so. To prove his point, he had me stand in the position I would have been in had I just finished throwing a punch to his midsection. In this position, my right arm was extended about stomach height with my hand formed into a fist, thumb facing the floor. My left hand, also formed into a fist, was pulled back to my side, thumb facing the ceiling. My instructor moved to my right side and placed his right hand on my extended right arm, his left hand over my back and around my left shoulder.

"Don't let me move you," he instructed. I took a little wider stance and made sure I was as centered as I could be. He then tried to pull me toward him using both hands. I felt very strong in my stance, and even though it was clear he was using quite a bit of muscle, he was unable to move me.

"Okay," he said, letting up the pressure he had been using to try to move me. "That was just muscle on muscle. Whoever is strongest has the advantage. Now I will do the same thing but will create an opening for my partner to move into." He placed his hands in the same positions on my body and then began trying to move me toward him. At first, there was no change from the first attempt. I felt very strong in my stance, and he was unable to move me. Then, as if some hidden force suddenly took over, my body seemed to weaken and I started falling toward him. Now, I hadn't seen him do anything different with his body, and I didn't feel him use any more pressure or muscle to accomplish what he had done. Still, I was unable to stop him from moving me.

"Did you see what I did?" our instructor asked the class. Everyone sat quiet, perhaps, like me, not wanting to admit they hadn't. "It's okay if you didn't," he continued. "What I did was very small. In fact, I didn't do anything on the outside of my body . . . just on the inside."

He asked me to take the same stance, which I did, and he placed his hands on me in the same manner as before. "No opening," he said as he tried to move me and couldn't. He paused and then said, "Now . . . an opening." Just as easy as the last time he created his opening, I began falling toward him. "Okay." He smiled. "Now I'll make it big so you can see it."

He again asked me to take my stance, and he again put his hands on me. "No opening," he said, trying to move me without success. "Now, an opening, but this time I'll make it big." Standing at my right side and with his right hand on my right arm and his left hand on my left shoulder, he turned his hips to the left, and immediately I began falling toward him just as I had before. "By turning my hips like this," he said, "I create a place for his body to go. If I stand static, I'm in his way and he can't go where I'm trying to put him."

We set up the same scenario again, and again he moved me with the same ease, but this time with only a little movement in his hips. The last time we set up the situation, he moved me without moving his hips at all. "The movement has become so small that it is all just on the inside," he said. "But it gets the same results because it still creates the same opening. It doesn't matter if the physical movement that creates the opening is big, or very small. The opening that is created because of it will always be the same."

It was that last statement that got me hooked: *It doesn't matter if the physical movement that creates the opening is big, or very small. The opening that is created because of it will always be the same.*

———

Now as I said earlier, openings are much easier to find or create when movement is present. But the concept our instructor presented to us that evening in class put a whole new perspective on the ideas of both openings *and* movement for me. In the past, I had always perceived openings as something overtly physical that could easily be seen or heard, such as a pause in a conversation or, as with the example I mentioned earlier, a boxer who has left a vital area of his body exposed to attack. I had also seen movement as—well, movement— something overtly physical that could be seen or heard.

The idea that both openings *and* movement could be so small that they could be unperceivable was an eye-opener for me to say the least, although not necessarily a concept that was totally foreign to me. For years we had been helping riders get their horses to change gaits by doing nothing more than thinking about changing rhythm in their minds. In other words, if a rider wanted to go from a walk (four-beat gait) to a trot (two-beat gait), I would ask him or her to count 1-2-3-4, 1-2-3-4, in time with him or her horse's feet as it moved. Then when they wanted to change gaits to the trot, I asked them to change the count and speed of the count to 1-2, 1-2, 1-2, which would be the rhythm and speed of the trot they were looking for. It was the same when going from a trot (two-beat gait) to a canter or lope (three-beat gait). I would ask them to count the two-beat gait in time with their horse's feet, 1-2, 1-2, 1-2, then start counting *1-2-3*, *1-2-3*, *1-2-3*, with an emphasis always on the first beat of the count as the first beat would be on the horse's outside hind foot, the foot the horse would need to use to push off to get to the canter.

This method has worked so well that many riders who tried it found after just a few attempts, they didn't need any physical aid whatsoever to achieve their transitions. Others found they might still need some sort of physical aid to get the transition, although usually not near the intensity of what they normally used. I believe the reason this method was so successful was that the changing of the rhythm by the rider created both unseen movement and openings perceivable and understood by the horse. After all, we humans think in terms of words, but I believe horses think and feel in terms of rhythm. If this is indeed the case, then it isn't that far of a stretch to think that a horse would pick up on a change of rhythm in the rider's body, even if that change is only at the level of a thought on the rider's part.

Along those same lines, something else we have been helping riders with for several years has been the idea of always presenting what you want from the horse *before* you actually ask for it. For instance, when most riders want their horse to walk forward, the very first thing they do is put some kind of an aid on the horse to get them to move. Yet seldom, if ever, is the rider actually thinking about moving themselves. In these cases, the rider is almost always thinking solely about getting the horse moving, but because *they* aren't moving (internally), they end up asking the horse to move into what could be considered both a physical and internal blockage on the rider's part. As a result, some of these folks end up getting sluggish transitions from halt to walk, some don't get any transition at all, and all of it due to the fact that no opening has been created for the horse to move into.

Instead, we've been helping folks understand how to present forward movement inside themselves first, *then* ask the horse to move. This usually helps in being able to get better, more responsive, and softer transitions from halt to walk. We've also stressed the same sort of thing for other movements that riders are looking for from their horses as well, such as turns on the forehand and haunches, side passing and/or leg yielding as well as stopping and backing. In the majority of these cases, by the rider doing nothing more than just thinking about "going first," or internally creating an opening for the horse to move into prior to actually applying an aid, the horse is almost always able to perform the task easier, softer, and with less effort all the way around.

Still, the idea that our instructor presented that night in class regarding openings and movement did add a new dimension to the concept. In particular, the thought that physical movement in a person's body could be reduced to the point of being nearly undetectable and still be just as effective in creating a physical opening for another individual was a real eye-opener for me. Of course my first thought when I came to this realization was if one human could have that much of an effect on another human with so little physical movement present, then our ability to effect a horse (in both positive and negative ways) using such little movement must be astronomical.

However, on the other side of the coin, I also realize that being able to provide openings to a horse with such minimal movement on our part doesn't necessarily come naturally for most folks. Not only that, but getting a horse to choose the opening once it is present may not be the easiest thing to do either. After all, I quickly came to realize when working on this concept in the dojo that to get good at creating the opening *and* getting our partner to move into it at the same time not only takes practice and lots of it but it also takes patience and self-control. Patience is needed when we feel the person (or horse) should be moving into the opening before the opening has actually formed, and the self-control is needed so we can stop ourselves from forcing the movement in our partner regardless of whether an opening is actually present or not.

I must say that the more thought I've given to this idea of openings, the more I've come to realize that whether the opening is something big and obvious, or the opening is something so small that it is literally undetectable to the human eye, it is indeed the openings in horsemanship (as well as life) that allow for positive movement in the direction we want to travel. Something else that I've come to understand about openings is that they can show up almost anywhere, they sometimes don't look or feel like we expect them to, and most important, if we aren't looking, we'll never find them.

All that being said, when it comes to understanding how these types of openings work, particularly in regard to how they work with horses, it seems that most humans may not be completely up to speed. Horses, on the other hand, appear to be masters of that understanding. When given an opportunity, a horse will not only find but also fit their entire body through an opening the size of a dime turned on its side, while us humans will often miss an opening big enough to drive a truck through.

The reason for this is that nature provides animals with an inherent understanding of openings as a way for both predators and prey to survive in the wild. For example, a prey animal will almost always zig and zag suddenly when being chased by a predator. While these maneuvers appear random, and sometimes they are, when watched closely it is easy to see that the zig often comes right as the predator is getting ready to commit themselves to a strike of one kind or another.

What most animals know, and humans have forgotten, is that whenever someone commits themselves completely to a strike of any kind, they are not only at their most powerful, but they are also at their most vulnerable. Total commitment doesn't allow for adjustments. A predator that commits to a kill strike can't adjust and therefore is actually creating a momentary opening for the prey to escape, providing the prey takes advantage of the opening by suddenly moving in the opposite direction to which the predator has committed.

On the other hand, the predator will also watch for an opening in their prey. This opening might come in the form of a momentary weakening or slowing in the prey's movement during a chase, or perhaps the prey zigging when they should have zagged. A more obvious opening might come in the form of a parent leaving its young unguarded, or an old, sick, or lame adult being left behind by the herd. In any case, openings are ever present in animal behavior, and their use and understanding have been honed by evolution over millions of years.

Now that isn't to say that us humans don't have the capability to understand and use openings, because we do. After all, we are animals too. However, as with so many of our inherent "animal" instincts, this one, too, has been pushed to the back burner due to our "civilized" way of living. But just because this particular instinct has inadvertently slowed down doesn't mean it doesn't exist, because it does. Not only that, but it can be brought back to life very easily and, with a little practice, can become a viable part of our entire life, not just our life with horses.

Still, being able to find, create, and use openings when working with horses can not only make our work with them much easier overall, but it can also allow for smoother communication in general and certainly more efficient *movement* in particular.

Even with all that being said, I truly believe developing the ability to see and use openings effectively is only one piece of what one might refer to as the "harmony in horsemanship" puzzle. When this idea of understanding openings is brought together with the understanding of two other similar ideas—making a *connection* with another individual, and the role that *distance* plays in overall communication—I believe it is then that harmony in horsemanship becomes a much less daunting concept for us. Of course I also believe that all of this might make working with us a little less tricky for our horse as well. And in the end, isn't that all that we're looking for anyway?

Chapter 9
Connections

_____

"You can go ahead and ride Diablo," my boss said, looking over the herd of horses that had just been brought in from off the mountain. It was Monday morning in mid-May, and the first day of what would ultimately be a four-day process of bringing the herd of about 125 head of horses off the 2,500-acre winter pasture and then taking them back to the ranch for the summer. I hadn't actually been on the schedule to help out on this particular gather. Instead I had been asked to stay behind and help with, and oversee, the fence repair in the big pasture at the ranch where the horses would be kept for the summer. However, just as

the crew was getting ready to leave the ranch and head to the pasture, the boss told me to throw my saddle in the back of one of the pickups and go along.

The winter pasture was down in the foothills, about thirty miles away from the ranch and just about halfway between the towns of Boulder and Lyons, Colorado. I had been on a number of these roundups and was normally put in charge of a small group of riders working the south end of the 2,500 acres of rocks, scrub brush, canyons, and valleys, while the boss usually took his riders to the north end.

As was the custom, the day started with the boss going up on the hill with a three-wheeled ATV—the kind that since have been discontinued due to their lack of stability and the countless injuries suffered by riders over the years when they flipped or rolled over—and would do a quick minigather of any horses that were close enough to the catch pen to bring in without a fuss. Out of those twenty or twenty-five horses that were brought in, the boss would then pick a horse for each rider, one that he felt would not only suit the rider but also be up to the task of climbing back up the mountain and working the big gather for the rest of the morning.

Several "good" gather horses had come in on the minigather that morning. These were usually horses that could easily be ridden off by themselves, had good feet and good stamina, and could stay with a band should the horses in it decide to bolt or try to outrun the riders, which did seem to happen from time to time, no matter how quietly we tried to move them. The horse the boss picked for me that day was a five-year-old sorrel paint gelding named Diablo.

I had never ridden the little horse before, but from the accounts of everybody who had, he was quick when you needed him to be and responsive almost to the point of being *too* responsive, if there is such a thing. He was a flashy horse that was just under fifteen hands, sturdy, with straight legs and good hard feet that made him an obvious choice when it came to picking a horse to use on the rough terrain the pasture provided.

I pulled him from the catch pen, tied him to one of the stock trailers we brought down from the ranch, groomed and saddled him, then waited for the rest of the crew to finish saddling their horses. As was often the case on these roundups, some of the horses—veterans of other gathers in past years—were a little fresh from having the winter off and not particularly interested in allowing themselves to be caught only to be saddled and ridden back up the mountain. As a result, catching and saddling them sometimes took a little longer than expected.

Still, within a relatively short time after the boss did the minigather, both crews, the northern crew that the boss would be riding with and the southern crew that I would be riding with, were all mounted and ready to start heading up the mountain. As is the case with so many old ranch properties in the west, this particular ranch where the horses were pastured for the winter was split in two unequal parts when the state put a highway directly through the property.

In this case, the home base where the barns, house, and catch pen were located was on the east side of the highway. The twenty-five-hundred-acre pasture where the horses were was on the west side. In order to get from the east side of the road to the west side, we needed to travel with our horses through a tunnel built under the road when the road was originally put in back in the 1930s. It was also this tunnel that the horses we would gather would need to pass through in order to get them into the catch pen.

Once on the western side of the road—the pasture side—my crew of four and I began heading south along the road. There were actually three main trails from the south end of the pasture that led to the upper meadows a thousand feet or so higher up, where at least some of the horses were sure to be. One of the trails went almost directly straight up the hill from the mouth of the tunnel. Another trail was about a third of a mile to the south, and the last trail was about a half mile farther south from there.

As we reached the first trail not far from the mouth of the tunnel, an interesting thing happened. I was looking at the crew and trying to figure out not only which of the riders had been on a gather before and might know that particular trail, but I was also picturing the trail in my mind as a way to help make a decision about which horses might do better during the climb to the top. The picture in my mind wasn't a static, nonmoving image like that of a photograph, but rather it was more like a video, a moving picture of the trail.

As was normal for me when trying to recall a certain familiar area I was passing through, I pictured this particular path as if I were actually riding it. The path began with the wide, relatively flat opening near where we stood. It then meandered up around the big rocks above us and through the growth of mountain mahogany where it then began to narrow. About there was also where the trail steepened and where the first of two sets of switchbacks started. Once past the switchbacks there was a stand of low-growing cedar, and beyond that, the trail narrowed once again, became rocky, and then there were the second set of switchbacks.

Beyond the switchbacks and near the top, the trail widened, and it eventually crested at the north end of the big flat meadow at the top of the mountain. There, a large outcropping of rocks would hide the riders from any horses that were in the meadow, and it would be there that I would have them wait until they saw me and the other members of the crew entering the meadow.

The interesting thing to me about this process was that as soon as the picture of the trail came into my mind, Diablo, the horse I was riding, turned and started up the trail. The more the various turns, rocks, switchbacks, and other landmarks on the trail passed in front of my mind's eye, the more determined he seemed to be to get up that trail. In fact, he actually became so determined that I had to redirect him several times using circles and figure eights just to keep him with the rest of the horses there at the trail head. However, it seemed the second I had finished the "virtual" trail ride in my mind and switched my focus back to where the crew was standing, Diablo stopped moving, dropped his head, and stood quietly.

After choosing the two crew members to take that trail to the top and sending them on their way, the other two crew members and myself continued south to the next trail. On our way, I began running the second trail through my mind. It began with three long steep switchbacks then wound through a number of big rocks, along the mountain mahogany bushes, down into a shallow ravine, back up the other side with two more switchbacks, entered the low-growing cedar, went around more rocks, and finally entered the meadow at the top of the mountain about midway between the north end where the first crew would be, and the southern end where I would eventually be.

The entire time I was running the picture of the trail in my mind, Diablo suddenly seemed to be having all kinds of trouble walking a straight line. He wandered to the left, then the right, then back to the left, then straight for a few steps, then back to the right and left. He then slowed for several steps then sped up for several more, swerved to the left and right before finally walking a straight Line. Just as I had reached the top of the trail in my mind, Diablo offered to stop.

Not really thinking anything of Diablo's apparent lack of steadiness or willingness to stop, I urged the little gelding forward, and before long we reached the second trailhead. I sent the other two riders up that trail, and Diablo and I continued on to the final trail that led to the upper meadow a half mile farther south. I didn't think too much about this trail as we approached due to the fact that this was the one we used most often to get up and down from the meadow and I was very familiar with it.

For his part, Diablo walked straight as an arrow all the way to the trailhead, then as if knowing exactly where we were going and what we were doing, he turned without me having to give him any direction whatsoever and began the climb to the top. Unlike the other two trails that were relatively steep and had a number of switchbacks along the way, this trail was more gradual and much less rocky. In fact, there were really only a couple places in the trail with rocks large enough to have to ride around, and over time the trails around those large rocks had become worn and braided.

Trail braiding happens when the original trail, which took a specific path around an obstacle, in this case a rock, begins to deepen and erode from overuse. When that occurs, the animals that use the path to get around the obstacle begin to use another path slightly to the side of the original. Eventually that path also becomes deep and eroded, and another path is needed. As years pass, this development of various trails occurs over and over until several paths around the same obstacle have been constructed, giving the impression that the trail has been "braided."

Over time the old, abandoned, or unused trails around the obstacle begin to fill back in with dirt and debris washed down from above. Then instead of having one good path around the obstacle, there end up being several not-so-good paths to choose from. Each time we came upon a braided area in the trail, I would look at each of the individual paths as we approached then pick the one I thought might be the best route. I noticed as I was deliberating, Diablo would slow his pace almost as if waiting for the decision to be made. The second I made my choice, Diablo would again pick up his pace and head directly for the route I had chosen without me having to give him any direction whatsoever.

The same thing happened as we reached the second braided area in the trail, as well as the third. Each time we approached an area that had more than one path and I needed to give some thought as to which one might be the best, Diablo would slow. As soon as I made my choice, he'd speed up and head directly for the line I'd picked. He would do the same thing as we came upon spots in the trail that were unusually rocky or difficult to navigate. I would pick a path around the obstacle I thought most prudent, and without having to so much as lift a rein, Diablo would go exactly to the area where I was looking.

Once up in the meadow, I could see there was a small band of horses about a half mile to the north but couldn't really see how many there were as a rise in the ground shielded some of the horses from view. Behind us was a large rock outcropping, the top of which was easily accessed by a nearby game trail, and just as I thought about going to the top of it to get a better view, Diablo turned around and, again, with no outward direction from me, headed toward the path.

Soon we were at the top of the outcropping, and I was able, from that vantage point, to survey nearly the entire meadow, almost all the way to the northernmost end where the two riders I had sent up the first trail were waiting. I could also see the second two riders waiting behind some rocks to the east of the meadow and roughly parallel to where the horses were grazing. This looked to be a relatively easy gather.

Diablo and I would move off the outcropping and head northwest, toward the little band that was in the middle of the meadow. As the horses began to move, the second group of riders would come from behind the rocks and funnel them farther north toward the riders' clear down on the north end. Those riders would then direct the herd east and down the path the first riders took to come up into the meadow. At the bottom of the trail, the horses we were moving would hopefully move through the tunnel quietly and into the catch pen on the other side of the road.

For the most part, once a band of veteran horses (horses that had been rounded up before) began moving downhill, they seemed to instinctively know they were going to be caught and easily gave up trying to run off or flee capture. However, if they bolted, split up, or tried to head north or south (escape to the west was cut off by the fence line at the westernmost edge of the meadow), which would keep them on top of the mountain, the chances would be very good we would be in for a long day of gathering and regathering until the herd decided on their own to give up and eventually move downhill. However, with the way the riders were positioned in the meadow that morning, all the normal escape routes were blocked and the only route open to the herd was the one we wanted them to use, so I felt confident the chances of this group escaping was actually relatively small.

Comfortable that this would be an easy group to gather, I decided to go ahead and start the push toward the north. At the very second I decided to move off the outcropping, Diablo turned and headed down toward the meadow. Up until that very moment, I had just assumed that Diablo's movement in whatever direction I was choosing without me having to supply him with any outward direction was nothing but coincidence. But as we moved into the meadow and I chose not only a course toward the herd (which was basically straight at them as the crow flies) and also a speed, a long working trot both of which Diablo somehow picked up on, I began to wonder if perhaps something else was going on between him and I.

Strange as it sounds, I got the impression Diablo was somehow reading my mind, or at the very least, trying to replicate through his actions almost exactly what I was thinking. I didn't pick up on it right away because when we were at the first trailhead when he tried to go up the trail as I was picturing the trail's path in my mind, I just assumed he was antsy and wanted to get to work. As I pictured the second trail in my mind while we approached it, I just assumed his awkward gait and (what appeared to be) unbalanced movement, was just that he hadn't been ridden in nine months, as he had been on winter pasture during that time.

However, as we began heading for the herd and I started looking back at all the things he had done that morning while we rode together, his actions began to take on a little different light. I thought about how, as we were approaching the second trail and I began running the trail through my mind, every time I pictured a turn in the trail, Diablo turned the same direction; when I thought about going down into the ravine, he slowed. When going up the other side of the ravine (in my mind), he sped up, and when in my mind I had reached the top of the trail, he stopped.

When we actually worked our way up the trail Diablo and I took into the meadow, each time I mentally hesitated so I could think about which of the braided trails we would take around an obstacle, he would hesitate. As soon as I picked the one I wanted to use, without outward direction from me, he sped up on his own and took the same trail. When I thought about climbing to the top of the outcropping once up in the meadow, he turned on his own and did so, and now he had picked the exact line and speed I wanted to use to get to the herd.

More as an experiment to see if my newfound suspicions about whether or not Diablo had actually somehow been "reading my mind" that morning, while heading for the herd, I began thinking about drifting three steps to the right. Sure enough, Diablo drifted to the right. I thought about drifting three steps to the left, and so Diablo did. I thought about slowing down, and he did. I thought about speeding up, and he did that too.

Not only that, but the rest of that morning as we went about the business of gathering horses off the mountain, I don't think I had to use either the reins to turn, stop, or slow him or my legs to encourage him to speed up more than a handful of times. All the rest of the times he seemed to be able to know where I wanted to go and what I wanted to do almost before I did.

Diablo was one of those horses that I can look back on and comfortably say that he helped change not only the way I look at horsemanship, but he also helped me stop and rethink the way we communicate with horses in general. He was the one that got me to wondering if we might be using more pressure than was needed or necessary when communicating with, or trying to teach, a horse the things we want them to know. I began wondering if there might actually be a way to communicate with horses using little more than a thought and still get the message across.

Still, back then, all I really knew for sure was that this particular horse apparently seemed to be able to read my mind. Everything else would take more than just a little looking into.

———

I'm not trying to give the impression that what happened between Diablo and myself is something special or out of the ordinary. In fact, my guess is that the vast majority of riders out there, regardless of experience level, breed of horse they ride, or even discipline they are into have, at one time or another, experienced something similar between them and their horse. This particular "phenomenon" is actually so common that at least one rider at nearly every clinic we have ever done has told me that at some point in the relationship with their horse they had thought about something they wanted their horse to do, and the horse just went ahead and did it.

For most of us humans, experiencing this type of thing with our horse seems a little out of the ordinary. After all, how can communication happen without words or some kind of physical contact or direction? Yet what we forget is that while most animals do communicate through sound and physical contact, the majority (including humans) also communicate on a much more subtle level as well. Of course living in the fast-paced, high tech world of instant written and verbal communication that we as humans live in today, it is difficult for us to imagine a time when humans were completely void of both. However, there was a time in our not-so-distant past when humans didn't have speech or the written word with which to communicate and instead relied on the same basic and relatively subtle forms of communication that all other animals still use.

When thinking about the subtle level at which horses are able to communicate with one another, a situation comes to mind with one of our own horses that I think illustrates this very well. One of my assistants had decided to buy a mare from one of the riders at one of our clinics that, by all accounts, did not play well with others. When placed in any herd, the mare quickly and forcefully took over by effectively terrorizing any and all horses in the herd that got in her way. When we got her home, we put her in a pen next to our herd and watched as she tried to push the others around even over the adjoining fence.

After a few days, things seemed to settle down, so we put her in with the herd to see how she'd do. She very quickly set about the business of exerting her dominance over the others and seemed to be doing a good job of it until one of the horses in our herd, a little dun quarter horse gelding by the name of Tuff, stepped in. Tuff, although just 14.2 hands, had been a breeding stallion until he was seven. That career came to a halt for him one night when he broke out of his pen and into the pen containing the ranch's broodmares, getting himself kicked in the face for his trouble. A few days later he was gelded.

We had owned him for about four years, and during that time Tuff's role in the herd had become that of peacekeeper, and it was a job he took pretty seriously. He didn't tolerate fights between herd members, and any disruptive behavior at all, such as the behavior the new mare brought to the herd, was met with a swift and very decisive reprimand. As long as he was in with the herd, the mare was pretty careful about what she did and how she did it. But if Tuff was taken from the herd to go out and work, she once again became a holy terror with whoever was left in the pen with her.

After a couple weeks of the mare's behavior disrupting the herd, we decided to get her out of the herd altogether and instead put her in a pen with Tuff. I wanted get her alone with Tuff for two reasons. One was that Tuff undoubtedly was able to handle the mare's behavior and hopefully by being with him she might learn a better way to get along with others, and the second and more important reason was to give the other members of the herd a break from her. Now while I wasn't exactly sure if having the mare in with Tuff would actually help her or not, what I did see happen between the two of them was something that kept me a little perplexed for quite a while.

I put the mare in a small pen with Tuff in the morning, and by midafternoon, this mare who had been terrorizing the other horses in the herd for over two weeks was standing quietly in the corner of the thirty-by-thirty-foot pen, head down, and sleeping while Tuff stood in the middle of the pen, also sleeping. When I went to throw the hay for their evening feeding, Tuff came quietly to the hay pile, and the mare excitedly came out of her corner toward the hay.

I was interested to see how this was going to play out because while the mare was fairly nasty with the other horses in the herd most of the time, she could be *extremely* nasty at feeding time. So much so that even Tuff had trouble with her occasionally. However, much to my surprise, there was absolutely no trouble to be had on this day. The mare left her corner, pinned her ears, and acted as if she was going to charge for the hay pile. She went about three steps then stopped dead in her tracks, eyes wide, ears pricked, and head up staring directly at Tuff. Tuff, on the other hand, was standing quietly, head down, eating from one of the three piles of hay I had put in the pen, and showed absolutely no outward sign whatsoever of even acknowledging that the mare was in the pen with him.

The mare watched him for a few brief seconds then turned and quietly walked back to her corner, dropped her head, and waited. I watched the whole thing very intently and saw absolutely nothing that told me Tuff had stopped the mare from coming toward the piles of hay, or that he had done anything at all to direct her back to her corner. But it was pretty clear by the mare's actions that something had happened between the two of them. I just had no idea what it was.

Intrigued by what I saw, I decided to spend as much time as I could over the next few weeks watching Tuff and the mare to see if I could pick up on what it was Tuff was doing to communicate his intentions to her. While I was somewhat surprised to see similar situations occur between the two on a number of occasions during that time, I was equally surprised to realize that no matter how hard I looked or how carefully I watched, I simply could not see what he was doing to influence her behavior.

My assistant spent about a year and a half with the mare, and while the mare's overall training under saddle improved, there was very limited change in her personality with other horses. Eventually, due to the mare's propensity to be a liability with and around other horses, my assistant decided to find another home for her. Still, the seemingly ultrasubtle interactions between the mare and Tuff stuck with me, and I continued to wonder what he had done to communicate with her and why it had been so effective.

———

Fast-forward five years, to a winter's evening at home when my wife Crissi was sitting in front of her laptop at the dining room table. She was just finishing up some research she had been doing on the effects of certain childhood trauma has on the brain when she called me over. "This is interesting," she said as she began reading the findings of a European study she had come across regarding a little known, but extremely important, function of the brain.

According to this particular report from 1996 in which researchers were studying the brain activity in monkeys, they found that when one monkey reached for a peanut, a certain part of its brain (a section where activity was not expected) became very active. That in and of itself, while interesting, was not as interesting as what was happening with another monkey's brain at the very same moment. A second monkey had been sitting some distance away and had done nothing more than watch the first monkey pick up the peanut. However, by simply observing the first monkey reach for the peanut, the same section of the second monkey's brain also began to activate. In other words, the second monkey was experiencing the same physical sensations that the first monkey was getting, even though the second monkey was doing nothing more than watching the first.

What these researchers had accidentally discovered from these two monkeys was a function in the brain driven by what they would later refer to as *mirror neurons*. In short, mirror neurons in the brain are the tools that animals (including humans) use to experience, imitate, and ultimately decipher behavior by watching another individual's actions, facial expressions, and movements. It turns out mirror neurons can be triggered by an animal observing an individual of the same species *or* by observing an individual from another species.

It is believed that this function in the brain is what we humans used when communicating with one another prior to the development of speech. It is also what allows us to feel in our own body something we are seeing happen to someone else. For instance, seeing someone accidentally hit themselves on the thumb with a hammer will elicit nearly the same reaction from the person watching as the person whose thumb was struck. At the very least, the person watching is bound to flinch or wince in pain as if they had also been struck.

In fact, I would wager to guess that for some people, just *reading* about a thumb getting struck by a hammer was enough to cause them to either look at their own thumb or perhaps even experience a vague sensation of one kind or another in their thumb.

Mirror neurons are what cause us to yawn when we see someone else yawning, feel happy when we see someone laughing, feel sad when we see someone crying, and feel compassion when we see someone in need. They are what helped us learn the intricate art of speech when we were very young by allowing us to read, decipher, and mimic the extremely subtle mouth movements used for speech patterns by our parents and others, as well as mimic body movement such as waving when someone waved to us or sticking out our tongue when someone did the same.

While allowing us to learn from others through mimicry of actions, or mirroring, seems to be a major role of mirror neurons, it is also widely believed that their primary function—when boiled down to its simplest form—is that they are dedicated specifically to allowing us to be able to understand the intentions and goals of others and then respond accordingly.

It should be pointed out here that the study of mirror neurons is still in its infancy and, to date, has been limited primarily to monkeys, humans, and some birds. However, it is assumed that most creatures that learn from watching others and/or communicate through facial expressions and body language (this would include horses) also possess mirror neurons in one form or another.

Some researchers believe that mirror neurons are so important to the various species living here on earth that they may actually be the key to harmonious living between *all* species. By understanding the intentions and goals of others simply by looking at one another, we can, and some might say already have, learned how to identify with others on a more global or even universal scale. In other words, it may be the mirror neurons in our brains that help keep us all, animals as well as humans, connected to one another in one way, shape, or form, and therefore also keep us all constantly striving to find ways to get along with one another.

I think most of us who have been around horses for a long time are constantly amazed at the subtlety with which they are able to communicate with one another, and with us when we choose to listen. I, for one, am also frequently impressed by how quickly horses are able to adapt their level of communication to fit the situation.

For instance, not long ago, we placed a horse in with our herd that had a history of violence toward others when put in with other horses. My guess was he wasn't violent because he was trying to be dominant but rather because he had relatively low self-confidence and perhaps just didn't know how to act when in a group. As a result, he had been striking out due to the fact that he felt he needed to defend himself.

As soon as we put the gelding in the pen with our horses, the entire herd of ten immediately surrounded and totally overwhelmed the new gelding to the point that he had no idea who to defend himself against, who to attack, or even which direction to turn. Somehow, I believe, the members of the herd saw something in him that told them this was the way this horse needed to be dealt with so he could learn the proper way to act right off the bat. The herd never gave him an opportunity to fight, strike, or even flee. He was unceremoniously put at the bottom of the pecking order, and within less than fifteen minutes, the new horse had not only accepted his place in the herd, but was also accepted *by* the herd.

In a more recent situation, we put an older, more self-confident gelding in with our horses, and the herd handled him much differently. In his case, all the horses confidently approached him, but did so one at a time, starting with Tuff, and then going down the line in order of position within the herd. The outcome was the same, meaning the gelding was relegated to the bottom of the pecking order. However, he, like the first horse, seemed to willingly accept this position, and everything stayed quiet and amiable.

It seemed clear in both cases that not only were the members of the herd able to read the new horses accurately but did so by interpreting body language so subtle it would be nearly imperceptible to us humans. By the same token, the new horses were able to under-stand what their position in the herd would be just by the way the herd communicated with them as well. Horses begin to learn this form of subtle communication from a very early age: both through watching others in the herd as they interact as well as the actual physical experience of it through daily herd dynamics.

We humans learn how to communicate with one another at a very subtle level from a very early age as well. By the time we are three or four years old, we have already become aware of and have learned how to read micro expressions in the people around us (expres-sions that are so small and occur so fast that most adults miss them), variations in voice inflections, and body language. However, unlike animals who always say what they mean and mean what they say, humans can look one way and act another. As a result, almost as soon as we learn how to read the expressions and body language of the people around us, we are also taught by those same people that what we are seeing and feeling isn't always accurate and so most of us begin to overlook the true subtleties of communication and ultimately learn how to believe what we *hear* instead of what we *see* or *feel*.

Horses, on the other hand, are just the opposite and for the most part rely more on what something looks like and feels like rather than what it sounds like. A horse's body language doesn't lie, and neither does its intent. When around one another, they take what each other is saying as gospel and respond accordingly. I believe most horses, when given a chance, will try to do the same with us and in fact often seem to go out of their way to search out the truth in our intent and show us the truth in theirs. The problem is, some-times we aren't even certain what our intent is in the first place, and we more times than not (if we are truthful with ourselves) aren't terribly interested in theirs. It is that breakdown in understanding intent that can make it difficult if not downright impossible for our horse to work with us in the effortless manner that many of us seek. As a result, we can sometimes feel disconnected from our horses and they from us.

Yet if we look at the big picture, it would appear truth in intent between horse and rider may very well be where that effortless connection we are all looking for with our horses comes from. The question many folks might ask then is, how do we develop truth in intent to begin with so that the connection we want can come through?

———————

During the demos we do prior to many of our clinics, I ask if any of the folks in attendance are interested in developing a connection with their horse. Usually, everybody raises their hand. When I then ask what "developing a connection" means, the answers I get are usually wide and varied. But when I ask people what it is that we have to do as riders to actually make that connection, most of the time things get pretty quiet. In other words, we know that we want to make a connection with our horse. We even have an idea of what that connection should look like and feel like. The only problem is we just don't know how to get there.

I used to think that there was something specific that we as riders needed to do to create the kind of connection we are talking about—a connection in which the lines of communication are so clear that aids and cues are nearly nonexistent and responses from our horses are virtually effortless. In fact, over the years, we have come up with a number of ideas to help guide riders on how to make such a connection. Some of these ideas had their foundation and basis in aikido and were the same ideas we would use in the dojo to connect with a partner during training and which, with practice, would help the partner respond effortlessly to a certain technique.

For the most part, the ideas we were showing riders did work with varying degrees of success. On the other side of the coin, however, these ideas also seemed to take a great deal of thought and practice on the rider's part. Then, as time passed, I began to look at this idea of developing a connection from a different perspective. It began to dawn on me that perhaps we had been looking at the whole thing a little backward.

The type of connection we are talking about, in its purest sense, is really nothing more or less than a form of very subtle communication between two individuals. Perhaps one way to look at this transfer of information might be to think of it as having a piece of flexible hose connecting horse and rider in which the information can effortlessly be passed back and forth between the two. If there is a blockage on either end of the hose, information can't be transferred. Because our minds are always so busy thinking about this, that, or the other, our end of the hose often becomes clogged with static, which not only makes it difficult for us to send information, but also makes it difficult to receive it. Yet when we are able to quiet our mind, it allows the hose to be clear of debris, which also allows for information to be exchanged more readily.

In the case of horse and rider, it could arguably be said that it is the horse that has the most experience in the type of subtle, clear communication we humans are trying to develop with them. After all, subtle communication is what they do for a living. Not only that, but unlike people, horses also haven't spent most of their lives inadvertently "dulling down" those skills in the first place, so their ability to send and receive information at the level we are talking about is not only instinctive to them, but it is also very natural.

It was then that I realized a horse like Diablo wasn't "reading" my mind because I was trying to connect to him. After all, at that time I wasn't. On that day, I was really only concerned with gathering the herd in the most productive way possible. Rather, what I have come to understand is that perhaps what was actually happening between the two of us was that Diablo was trying to do what came naturally to *him*. He was "connecting" with me.

On the day I rode Diablo, I wasn't "training" or otherwise focused on getting something specific from him, which (using our hose metaphor) ultimately allowed for an unclogged passage in which information could flow. As a result, I may have unknowingly created an opening in myself that allowed him to *feel* what I was *thinking*. As a result, if I thought turn, he turned; if I thought slow down or speed up, he did; and if I thought stop, he did that too.

Perhaps my thoughts triggered micro impulses in my body that Diablo not only picked up on but also engaged the mirror neurons in his brain, which ultimately turned my thought into his action. Perhaps it was something else altogether. Either way, he had apparently connected with me at a level that I previously had thought was only reserved for horse-to-horse communication, the kind that was exhibited between Tuff and the mare or the herd and the new geldings.

After years of trying to find ways of helping riders connect to their horse, it finally came to me that perhaps what we should be doing instead is simply allowing them to connect to us. After all, not only are they obviously better at it than we are, but when given the opportunity, they also seem to search it out with every rider and in nearly every situation!

In one recent clinic, we had a rider whose horse, a 17-hands, 1,300-pound Warmblood who had only been under saddle for two years, would charge through transitions, was difficult to slow down after the canter, was very heavy on the forehand and in the bridle, and had difficulty turning. We literally did nothing more than ask the rider to think about the things she wanted her horse to do differently, and what that difference would look and feel like, then added minimal physical direction; and by the end of the first day, the big mare was already turning better, transitioning softer, and was able to regulate her speed after the canter. By the second day, and with almost no rein contact whatsoever, not only was the mare off her forehand, but she was also traveling in self-carriage most of the time, was able to perform the beginnings of passage (an elevated trot with minimal forward movement), she was performing lateral work (leg yields) without the use of leg aids, and her transitions both up and down were effortless, smooth, and soft.

In the same clinic was a woman who was relatively new into riding and whose quarter horse gelding was spooky, difficult to control in faster gaits, and seemed unusually defensive any time his rider used any leg cues on him whatsoever. Again, by doing little more than changing the way the woman *thought* about what she wanted from horse and how she wanted him to do it, along with helping the woman breathe a little better than she had been, and making a few minor adjustments in her aids, her horse almost immediately became much quieter, calmer, and easier to work with. She, too, was very quickly able to develop transitions with her horse without the use of visible cues, effortlessly regulate speed within a gait, and achieve lateral movements without the use of leg aids.

Now I realize that this kind of thing might be hard for some folks to imagine, especially if they've been struggling with behavioral or performance issues with their horses. And the truth is, there are horses and riders that we come in contact with who, for one reason or another, do need more guidance and structure to the work we do with them in order to overcome the issues they may be having or in order to help develop a better connection between the two.

However, that doesn't alter the fact that the vast majority of riders we see, regardless of skill level or discipline, end up with very similar results as the two women I mentioned. We are finding more and more that by the rider doing little more than offering the horse true clarity in intent, along with softening the intensity of, or in some cases even eliminating cues, the horse seems not only to be able to connect to the rider on an extremely subtle level, but the development of effortless responses appears to be immediate and lasting.

———————

Crissi and I were demonstrating this idea of developing a connection through clarity of intent with three separate riders during a session we were teaching at a big horse expo a couple years back. Within just a few minutes, each rider was able to achieve the kind of connection we are talking about with their horse, which quickly led to each rider being able to do transitions without having to apply any aids whatsoever. During the middle of the session, I asked the audience seated in the coliseum if there were any questions. A number of people raised their hands, and when I called on a woman about midway up the grandstands, she stood up and asked, "Is it *really* that easy?"

"Yes," I responded. Several people raised their hands again, and I turned and picked a man on the other side of the arena. "Yes, sir?" I said, pointing to him.

"Is it really that easy?" he asked, too.

It dawned on me that I hadn't repeated the first woman's question, so although I had answered it, nobody else in the vast building had heard what she said. "Let me repeat the question," I said over the microphone. "He asked if it's really that easy." I nodded. "Yes, it is." I turned to point to another woman sitting nearby the man. "Or at least it sure appears to be," I added. A chuckle rippled through the crowd.

Interestingly enough, when we had finished the session and I again asked the crowd if there were any questions, several people, one right after another, raised their hands and asked that very same thing. *Is it really that easy?* I can sure understand why people would wonder about that. After all, traditionally, anything that has to do with riding or working with horses has always had some degree of difficulty associated with it. Yet when we stop to see the extreme subtlety with which horses are able to communicate with one another, and the ease and grace with which they are able to move when they aren't encumbered by a rider, one has to wonder why getting a horse to do anything under saddle would be so difficult in the first place.

It seems to me that throughout the years, man has spent so much time trying to physically manipulate the horse into effortlessly performing the things they can already do naturally, that we may have gotten away from the one thing that might actually help us accomplish that effortlessness in the first place. Placing our focus on allowing the horse to link up with us through our openness and clarity of intent instead of the constant focus on physical manipulation seems to be the key. Don't get me wrong here; I am certainly not saying that physical cues and aids are not needed or warranted for communication and performance between horse and rider, because they are. It's just that it is becoming increasingly more clear (and science seems to bear this out through the discovery of mirror neurons) that influencing the inside of the horse through the rider's thought and intent is not only possible but also pretty simple and relatively easy to do.

After all, if all creatures *are* hardwired by nature to connect to one another, i.e., through the mirror neurons in our brains, and we all have the ability at some level to understand the intentions and goals of others, then perhaps we've been missing the boat when it comes to subtle communication. Again, I want to be clear here that I'm not trying to imply that riding through *thought* alone is the only way to go. I think at this point that might be a little premature and perhaps even a little unrealistic. However, I do think if we couple our own openness and clarity of intent with the technique we are already using, or perhaps even make some minor adjustments in that technique if needed, getting to the effortlessness in communication with horses we are looking for might actually be a little closer at hand than we think.

Chapter 10
Distance/Spacing

All three of our geldings lazily walked up to the gate when they saw Crissi and I show up. Rocky was first to get there followed by Tuff. Mic, the five-year-old buckskin I had been spending most of my time clinicing with lately, brought up the rear. Rocky and Tuff stopped relatively close to the gate while Mic stopped about ten feet to the right of the gate and about six feet from the heavy metal pipe fence the gate was attached to. He stood at a slight angle to the fence, facing the gate. On the other side of that fence and in a pen next to the one our horses were in was a 17-hands, 1,800-pound Belgian draft horse gelding.

The big horse was clear across the other side of his pen munching on a small pile of hay when our horses walked up. However, no sooner had they all stopped near the gate than the Belgian unexpectedly wheeled and charged toward them. With ears pinned, nostrils flared, and teeth gnashing, the big sorrel gelding stampeded across his pen and headed straight for Mic, who was still standing quietly, head down, and hind foot cocked. The Belgian crashed violently into the heavy fence chest first and reached as far over the top rail as he could in an apparent attempt to get to Mic.

As surprising to me as the big horse's attack was, I was even more surprised by Mic's response. Or perhaps a better way to say that might be that I was more surprised by Mic's *non*response. With 1,800 pounds of extremely upset horse-zilla bearing down on him, and the big horse making a first-class attack over the fence, Mic never flinched. He didn't bat an eye, never pinned an ear, and didn't even uncock his hind foot.

The Belgian, on the other hand, pushed relentlessly on the immovable metal fence and stretched as far as he possibly could, trying to get his teeth on Mic. But it didn't matter how hard he pushed or how far he stretched, the big horse always fell about a quarter inch short of making any kind of contact with him whatsoever. At first I wondered why Mic didn't do anything to defend himself, or why he didn't try to move farther out of range. But then the longer I watched this interaction, the more I realized there was simply no need for Mic to get upset or defend himself. Somehow he already knew the big horse couldn't reach him. It was then that it dawned on me that it didn't matter if the gap between him and his assailant was a quarter inch or a quarter mile. Either way, he wasn't going to be harmed because he was out of range and ultimately in control of the situation, not the Belgian.

I had to smile at this realization because the principle that Mic seemed to know instinctively had actually taken me years of training in the dojo to even begin to understand. *Whoever controls the distance, controls the situation.*

––––––––––

Ever since I began my training in aikido, I had been hearing from my instructors about the importance of *distance* in relation to one's opponent. This distance between forces is referred to in Japanese as *ma-ai* (pronounced *my-i*) and it is widely believed in martial arts circles that the mastery of ma-ai and all it entails leads to the mastery of the art. However, when I was first starting out, the study of ma-ai was just one more thing in a long line of things that had limited meaning to me, and to be honest, back then I wasn't sure what the big deal was to begin with. After all, how hard could it be to get the correct distance when facing off with an opponent anyway? It seemed simple enough to me. If your opponent wants to hit you, you just make sure he doesn't. There . . . done deal.

When it comes to my experience with aikido, as I moved up the ranks I began to understand more—as happens with so many things—and I slowly came to understand just how truly important correct ma-ai is. I began to see that when the distance was off between an attacking partner and myself, so was my technique. The reason my technique would be off, as I would eventually come to appreciate, was because ma-ai wasn't just about the physical distance between two individuals, as I had always believed. Ma-ai was also about what transpired within that space, and that was the part I had been overlooking.

Now before going any further, it may be worthwhile to point out that the meaning of ma-ai is often translated into just one word, that being either 'space' or 'distance.' Because of this, for a very long time I thought ma-ai simply referred to the physical distance between two training partners. In other words, if you were relatively close to an attacking partner, you could usually get to them in time and your technique would work fairly well. However, if you were too far away from an attacking partner, or too close for that matter, chances were very good that your technique would be off, sometimes off pretty dramatically.

However, what I didn't really understand during that time was that ma-ai could actually be considered a phrase, not a word. When broken down, *ma* actually means 'space' or 'interval,' and *ai* means 'joining' or 'coming together'. So *ma-ai* actually means the "joining of *shared space*," not just physical distance, as I had always believed. Perhaps another way to look at it might be that ma-ai is the coming together of time, space, and energy between two individuals.

Now I realize this may seem like a trivial difference in the translation between two languages, but for me it was a missing piece of a relatively big puzzle (both in aikido and in horsemanship). You see, distance between two individuals is still just distance, particularly if the two individuals aren't brought together somehow. And if the two individuals *are* brought together, such as during an attack, or perhaps in the case of a horse that doesn't understand boundaries with people, then whoever is in control of ma-ai (time, space, and energy) usually ends up in control of the situation.

Everything happened so fast that it was over before I even knew it, and as the gelding brushed safely past me in a panicked gallop, something my aikido instructor said to me in class just a few weeks earlier flashed through my mind. "Sometimes the difference between getting hurt or not when someone attacks is little more than the thickness of a piece of paper," he had told me. "If you don't want to get hurt, just make sure you're on the correct side of the paper."

That evening in class we had been working on an exercise in which uke would throw a punch at nage's midsection, and nage would turn his body at the very last second to avoid being hit. It was an exercise we hadn't really done before, and surprisingly, most of the students were having trouble with it, myself included. It was strange, too, because the exercise sure seemed simple enough . . . just turn before you get hit. (In Japanese, the timing of this turn is referred to as *de-ai*.) But sometimes even the simplest of things can be surprisingly difficult.

Nearly everyone in class that night seemed to be having the same issues. Sometimes we would turn too late and the punch would hit us in the stomach. Other times we would turn too soon, allowing uke to track the movement of our turn, and again, he would be able to hit us. Still other times we might jump out of the way of the punch like a matador moving out of the way of a charging bull, and sometimes we wouldn't move at all. After getting hit for the third time in a row by my partner, our instructor came over and began talking to me about the idea behind the concept we were working on.

He spoke about how the Japanese refer to this particular concept of staying safe as *kami shito* (pronounced, *come-i sheet-o*). Basically, what kami shito boils down to for warriors is the distance between life and death and how oftentimes that distance is no more than the thickness of a piece of paper. It is the management of that very small distance that can, and often does, make the difference between living or dying or being injured or not.

On this particular day, I learned firsthand about the management of that distance. We had just turned the gelding, who the owner had said was very difficult to catch, loose in the round pen. After removing his halter and letting him go, I had moved to the middle of the pen to give him an opportunity to run around a little if he wanted to before starting to work with him on his catching issue. He had only made a couple laps at a fairly easy lope when someone opened the lid on a nearby Dumpster to throw something away and then let the lid slam shut after having done so. By coincidence, the gelding just happened to be passing in between the Dumpster and me just as the lid crashed down, which caused him to spook, spin, and charge directly toward me.

The panicked gelding covered the ground between the round pen fence and where I was standing much faster than I would have thought possible, and I don't recall moving out of his way before he hit me, but that was exactly what I had done. The exercise we had worked on in the dojo just a few weeks before had somehow kicked in and allowed me to turn my body and move harmlessly out of his way just as it seemed inevitable he was going to run me over. One second we were face-to-face with the gelding bearing down on me, the next I was facing his side as he rushed past, less than a half inch to spare between us.

It was only then that I truly began to understand the importance of kami shito in relation to the joining of shared space. It was the exact same lesson Mic was able to illustrate so well when dealing with the big Belgian draft horse that was charging him. Whether working with people or working with horses, *"If you don't want to get hurt, just make sure you're on the correct side of the paper."*

When one stops to think about it, ma-ai, or the joining of shared space occurs in all aspects of horsemanship. It occurs between one horse and another out in the pasture and between our horses and us when we go to catch them. It occurs when we're leading them from one place to another, and it's in the lead rope that we use when we do so. It's in the relationship between our body and theirs when we're grooming them, the relationship between the bit and their teeth both when bridling them and when they're being ridden, and it's in the relationship between our legs and their sides when we're giving aids or cues.

Proper ma-ai is in the relationship between where we stand and where they stand when we put the saddle on their back. It's in the relationship between where we stand and where they walk when loading them into a trailer, the distance between us and other horses when in the show ring or on the trail, us and them when lunging, and the horse and an obstacle when jumping.

Ma-ai is indeed in every aspect of horses and horsemanship. However, I believe the one aspect of ma-ai that may be the single most important when it comes to the relationship between horses and riders is the space between the rider's hand and the horse's mouth.

When I first began doing clinics, I was amazed at the number of people who showed up to ride who seemed to be, for one reason or another, afraid to use their reins. Many of these folks rode with reins so loose that they would end up with two or three feet of slack between their hand and their horse's mouth. Now I certainly don't see much of a problem with this sort of thing when the horse is fairly well educated, understands its job, and knows how to respond to a rider's request. But the horses we were seeing didn't really fit into that category.

The horses we were seeing back then, and to some extent still see today, were having trouble with relatively basic things such as stopping, turning, and even doing something as simple as walking a straight line. The one thing all these horses had in common were the length of rein they were being ridden with was so long the rider simply couldn't get a cue or correction to them quickly enough to be of any real help. In other words, the rider had inadvertently turned control of ma-ai over to the horse.

Obviously, the rider hadn't intended to turn control over to the horse. Most were riding with long reins for what they thought were very good reasons. Some would tell us they didn't think their hands were good enough to have contact with the horse via the reins. Others would say they didn't want to hurt the horse's mouth by accidentally pulling on them while still others had been taught by one instructor or another that using the reins was somehow a "bad" thing. Unfortunately, regardless of the reason, by riding with such a long rein, each individual had inadvertently given up control of those three basic elements that make up ma-ai—time, space, and energy—ultimately helping to create discord and friction between them and their horse.

I remember one such rider who said he was having trouble getting his horse to go past a gate anytime he rode the little gelding in an arena. I had asked the man to ride the gelding past the gate in the arena we were working in that day, some sixty feet away from where we were chatting, so I could get a look at what was going on. The man mounted up and headed toward the gate. As the pair got to within about thirty feet of the gate, the gelding slowly began to pick up speed. He quickly turned his full focus toward the gate, which was to their left, and headed straight for it.

The rider, who had a good two and a half feet of slack in his reins, began to lift the right rein in an apparent attempt to make contact with the bit and turn the gelding. Within seconds, however, and with the rider being unable to apply any kind of meaningful pressure on the bit whatsoever, the pair closed in on the gate. Still trying to make a connection with the horse, the man had his right rein up above his head and was stretching to get the last little bit of slack from the rein. Still, it wasn't until after the horse literally walked right into the closed gate that he finally made contact with the horse. Of course, by that time it was way too late, and not only had the horse made it to his objective, he was also standing quite contentedly with his head and neck over the gate and his chest pressed tightly up against it.

Unfortunately, the rider had predetermined the outcome of this situation almost as soon as he threw a leg over the horse's back. No sooner had his backside landed in the saddle than he built all that slack in his reins and effectively turned all control of time, space, and energy between him and his horse over to the gelding. The horse was then able to easily travel the distance between where the rider mounted up and where the gate was in less than thirty seconds.

While all that was going on, the rider missed a number of opportunities to redirect the horse simply because the space between the rider's hand and the horse's mouth was so great that it took too much time to get all the slack from the rein, and as a result, the energy he used to do so was wasted. The horse had had complete control of ma-ai. In this case, he not only had control of the space between himself and the rider's hand, but he also had control of the space between where the rider mounted up and the gate where they eventually ended up.

I asked the rider to shorten his reins to the point where nearly all of the slack was gone then turn his horse away from the gate and come back to his original position in the arena. Much to his surprise, once he had shortened the reins, the horse came away from the gate willingly and without hesitation, whereas when his reins were long, he couldn't get the horse's head turned at all. Then without building any of the slack back in the reins, I asked him to turn the gelding around and ride back past the gate. This time, the gelding began to speed up and look toward the gate in about the same place he had the first time, but because the rider was able to make contact with him and give direction *before* the horse's thought turned into an action, the horse easily turned away from the gate and walked quietly past.

What this rider had felt was the difference between the *joining of shared space* and the complete giving up, or surrendering, of that same space. I like to compare the joining of shared space, ma-ai, with something I used to practice a lot when I was a kid. When I was young, one of my favorite things to do on the playground in the schoolyard across the street from our house was to stand on the middle of the teeter-totter and see if I could bring the board into perfect balance with both ends staying an equal distance off the ground. When I first began attempting this, getting the thing to balance in such a way wasn't easy. I found I had to get just the right amount of weight in each foot and also have each foot just the right distance from the center pivot point in order to pull it off. The board was always made out of heavy pine that weighed just as much, if not more than, I did and was usually painted shiny forest green, which made the board just a tad slippery. Still, with time and practice, I was eventually able to get the teeter-totter in balance, and the more I practiced, the quicker I could get it there.

However, once the big, heavy board was in balance, the trick was then in trying to keep it in balance. It never failed that the slightest shift of my weight or even a casual light breeze would be all it would take to get the board tipping one way or another. Of course we should keep in mind here that one side of all teeter-totters is always slightly longer than the other, which keeps them perpetually out of balance to begin with. Still, what I noticed was that regardless of the reason for it tipping, if I didn't allow the ends of the board to drop too much, or if I didn't allow my body to get too rigid, it was always much easier to bring the board back in balance once out. On the other side of the coin, I also noticed that the farther I allowed the board to tip in one direction or another, not only was it much more difficult to bring it back in balance, but I would undoubtedly need to use more effort and find myself getting more and more rigid in order to do so.

For me, this is the secret to the development of good ma-ai, and it was what the rider found when trying to take his horse past the gate. The closer he was to the "pivot" point, the point at which either he would retain control of the situation or turn the control over to the horse, the easier it was for him to keep things in balance and give direction, *and* the easier it was for the horse to take direction. The farther away he moved from that point, the more difficult staying in balance, and ultimately giving and receiving direction, became.

I should probably take a minute here and talk a little about the pivot point I just mentioned. Like the teeter-totter that sits on a point of balance in order for it to become functional, shared space also has what we might refer to as a point of balance as well. Let's say, just for argument's sake, that shared space between horse and rider through the reins works like the balance point of a teeter-totter. Using a numerical scale, when a horse is soft and willingly able to give to the bit in a natural and comfortable headset, then that natural position might be referred to as 0, or the point of balance between the rider's hands and the horse's mouth. If the horse's head moves away from the rider's hands, the scale increases from 0 to .5, then to 1, then 1.5, and so on up the scale, depending on how far away from the rider's hands the horse's head travels.

Consequently, if the horse's head is at 0 and the rider pulls on the bit, causing the horse's head to unwillingly go toward the rider, the scale would then go from 0 to .5, to -1, then -1.5, and so on. For our purposes, we could say that the shared space between horse and rider lies between the numbers 1 and −1 on that scale. It is my belief that inside those numbers is where the physical, and even to some extent emotional, connection and balance between horse and rider lives. Between those numbers, the balance can be tipped a little in one direction or another off 0 and still be brought back with relative ease. Any farther outside those numbers, however, and regaining that balance begins to get more and more difficult, just like trying to balance in the middle of a teeter-totter when the board has tipped too much.

This, I believe, is why things get so difficult for people (and their horses) when an exaggerated loose rein, or for that matter, when too much contact on the reins, is used. Both can, and often do, provide a lack of balance between the pair. This is why when either the horse *or* rider has trouble finding, developing, or staying within the shared space that mutual softness provides, everything simply becomes much more difficult for both parties.

Yet when riders and horses work together toward the same goal—mutual softness within shared space—and the better they become at developing and maintaining that softness, eventually a large shared space is no longer needed. In fact, it has been my experience that as time goes on, and as that space begins to shrink through understanding and practice, the shared space between horse and rider can actually become so small that physical aids are no longer needed to convey intent.

Still, before any of that can happen, it is important that we first develop a good understanding of shared space, how to move into or out of it, and when necessary, even how to direct or control it.

———————

Some people don't like the answer I give them when they ask me what is needed in order to develop an understanding for the joining of shared space in horsemanship. Probably because the answer is the same as it is when training in the dojo. It starts with listening to our intuition. In aikido, it usually doesn't take too long to realize that something is off when a certain technique consistently isn't working properly or isn't getting the desired response. Almost right away, that little intuitive voice in our head begins to tell us that something needs to change in order for the situation to get better. However, because we are already so focused on trying to get the technique correct, we all but ignore the little voice that is usually pointing us directly toward the solution.

It took me years into my aikido training to realize that if I let it, my body would automatically make the necessary adjustments in ma-ai. If I was working on a technique and my little voice was telling me *something's not right*, all I had to do was allow my body to line itself up with my uke, and nine times out of ten, my distance would either be correct, or would be very close to it. You see, in these types of situations, the body already knows what to do to keep itself safe. The problem is, being higher-thinking mammals, we assume we know more than our body does, so we try to override the body and "reason," or think our way out of it.

It is the same with horsemanship. I would say that in the vast majority of riders we see, one of the first things I ask them to do is either shorten or lengthen their reins because the length of rein they're currently using is either causing or adding to the problems they are having. In other words, I'm asking them to adjust the ma-ai between them and their horses, and these relatively small adjustments usually begin to create a positive change between the pair in a matter of minutes. Many of these riders have come to me later and told me that they knew something wasn't right, they just had no idea it would be something as simple as *that!*

The truth of the matter is, they probably did know. Or at the very least, their body probably did. The problem was, they were trying to think their way through the technical part of the situation rather than relying on what their body was trying to tell them about the *feel* of the situation. Our body is a pretty amazing tool that can actually keep us out of all kinds of trouble if we let it. Research has proven that the body becomes aware of potentially dangerous or harmful things and situations long before we are consciously aware of them. It also starts looking for solutions to the situation by getting itself ready to act or react—again, often before we are consciously aware there's even a problem.

That nagging feeling we get when something just doesn't feel right to us is actually part of an alarm system that nature has installed in all animals, not just humans. The only difference is, almost all other animals on the planet listen to the alarm; humans usually don't. After all, how many times have we heard a friend or colleague or family member say something like, *I knew something wasn't right, but I went ahead and did it anyway?* Of course that statement is usually followed by *and that's when I broke my leg,* or *hit my head,* or *fell off my horse,* or *drove into the ditch,* or any number of other unfortunate and probably avoidable results of not listening to that little warning that our internal alarm system sent our way.

It's like that old joke about the man who is standing on his porch while floodwaters are rising. When the police show up in a squad car to take him to safety, he refuses to go, saying that God will save him. Some time later, with the floodwaters rising fast, he's on the second floor of his house hanging out the window when rescuers in a boat show up. "Get in," they say. "We'll get you out of here." Again, he refuses, saying that God will save him. Soon, he's up on the roof with the water lapping at his heels. Men in a helicopter fly over him and drop him a ladder. Once more he refuses, saying God will save him. Eventually the floodwaters overtake him and he drowns. Standing at the pearly gate, he meets God. "Lord," he says. "May I ask a question?"

"Of course," God says.

"Please don't get me wrong because I'm very happy to be here," the man starts. "But I'm confused. I've always put all my faith in you, and in fact, I truly believed that you'd come and save me from the flood. Why did you let me drown?"

God smiles. "I sent you a car, a boat, and a helicopter. What else did you want?"

The point being, as is the case with most things in horsemanship, the solutions to a lot of our issues are often right there in front of us. The only problem is we are usually looking so hard in some other direction that we never see them. Paying attention to our intuition can allow us the freedom to step back from a situation and perhaps look at it from a different perspective. In other words, it can allow us the opportunity to create some distance between us and what's going on, which in turn can, and often does, bring the big picture into focus.

For instance, when I first began doing clinics, I rode almost all of my student's horses for them. If a problem came up, I would rather just get on and sort it out than take the time to try and teach the rider how to do it. However, several years back, I realized many of my students would return to our next clinic in their area still having the same issues with their horses. Obviously, something wasn't right. The students should have been progressing, not showing up year after year with the same issues. Eventually, it dawned on me that although

I might have been able to get on and achieve the desired response from the horse, most times the rider still wasn't able to. I figured the only way that was going to change was for me to stay on the ground and start finding ways to coach the riders through whatever the situation was that they were having with their horse, rather than just getting on and taking care of it for them.

I have to admit that watching riders struggle with their horses while they were going through the learning process was a difficult thing for me to do at first. However, I have since come to the understanding that creating that space between myself and the student (them on the horse, me on the ground) not only allowed me to see and learn much more as an instructor than I might have had I been doing all the work from on top of the horse, but it also gave riders the opportunity and skills to work through the issues themselves.

In another, more recent example of both listening to intuition and creating distance because of it, we were doing a series of summer clinics at our friend's place up in New Hampshire. We had already finished one weeklong clinic and were on the first day of our second weeklong clinic when something interesting happened. When Crissi and I pulled our horses from the pasture that morning, I noticed Rocky, the horse I would be using that day, seemed a little out of sorts. Rocky could be a little jumpy from time to time when on the road, but it was never anything serious, and as we loaded he and Crissi's horse, Bree, into the trailer to take them to the clinic venue, I figured he'd probably work out whatever was bothering him by the time we got there.

Unfortunately, Rocky didn't seem any better by the time I unloaded him and went to grooming and tacking him up. In fact, the longer he stood at the trailer, the more agitated he seemed to get. So much so that by the time I went to take him the arena so we could go to work, one of those little internal warning alarms began to go off in the back of my head. Like most everybody else, I suppose, I have spent more than my fair share of time ignoring that intuitive feeling of impending trouble that pops up from time to time, and ultimately paying for it later. But lucky for me (at least on that day), I chose to stop and pay attention to what I was feeling instead of charging forward into the potential abyss that lay ahead.

About halfway to the arena, with Rocky bouncing around on the end of the lead rope like one of those little chrome balls in a pinball game, I went back to the trailer and pulled out our twenty-eight-foot lunge line. I took Rocky back to the arena, snapped the end of the line to his halter, and asked him to trot a circle around me. Now it might be interesting to note here that in the four years that we had owned Rocky, I had never once done any kind of lunging with him. He was a good saddle horse when I got him and I never really saw or had any need to do so. Yet on this day, for some reason, it just seemed like the thing to do.

Rocky shook his head and snorted as I asked him to begin trotting, took about five steps, then came completely untrained. He grabbed his tail, clenching it tightly to his hind-quarters, broke in half, and went to jumping like he was in the running for NFR Bucking Horse of the Year. I asked him to move out to the end of the lunge line and speed up to a canter, which he did between bucks, jumps, and snorts. After a couple laps, he smoothed out and finally began cantering with some rhythm, and after a few more laps, he began breathing. It was then that his head dropped, his body relaxed, and he began moving like nothing had been wrong in the first place.

I let him lope a few more circles then reversed direction and let him head off for a few laps the other way. Less than five minutes from when the whole thing began, I was on him, and we were back in the arena ready for the day. Now the interesting thing here was that Rocky had never offered anything even close to that kind of behavior during the entire time we'd owned him, and he hasn't offered anything like it since. Yet on that day, for whatever reason, it was what he needed to do.

By listening to my intuition and putting a little distance between him and me, he was able to do what he needed to do, and in turn, I didn't need to worry about getting in the middle of a storm I didn't want to be in in the first place. I must admit, however, there was a time when ego may have gotten the best of me in a situation like that. After all, a clinician's horse isn't supposed to act up, particularly when they're in a working environment. As a result, I may have actually closed the space between Rocky and me by getting on him instead of widening the space between us by staying on the ground and lunging him. Of course there's no telling what might have happened had I chosen that direction instead of the one I did. But the fact still remains that nobody got hurt, no animosity had to get built up, and everybody was able to do what needed to get done—Rocky was able to blow off steam, and I was able to do my job for the day.

The interesting thing here, at least for me, is just like when I decided to coach students from a distance instead of riding their horses for them, Rocky and I were still working within a shared space. But lunging Rocky instead of riding him allowed for a bigger picture to develop in which nothing spun out of control, everybody could stay safe, and positive growth could happen.

Like so many other things in life, we seldom give the distance we use or share with one another very much thought, especially when it comes to horsemanship. Unless, of course, that distance is somehow causing some kind of problem, such as our horse constantly bumping into us or running past us when we are leading them, or our horse staying just out of reach when we try to catch him or when we can't get them turned or stopped when we're riding them. When problems like that show up, then we start giving distance all kinds of thought! I should know because I was right there in the same boat not too long ago.

However, the more time I have spent studying ma-ai over the years, both in terms of horsemanship and in terms of martial arts, the more I see how the mastering of ma-ai is indeed tied directly to the mastering of the art. At the very least, it's clear to see how having the correct distance and being able to manage the space between two individuals is a huge step in the development of harmonious interaction.

On the other hand, it's just as easy to see that when that distance and management of space is off, even just a little, everything becomes more difficult and in some cases can even mean the difference between life and death. Now I realize that may sound a little dramatic, but just as an illustration of how important distance is to life as we know it, most scientists agree that if the earth were just a few miles closer to the sun, or a few miles farther away, life on our planet might not even exist at all!

To think that just a few miles difference one way or another in the total vastness of the universe could mean the difference between whether or not life on our planet exists or not is a wondrous thought to me. Time, space, and energy had to come together at just right moment and with just the right amount of force for the harmony that we now know as life to ultimately be created.

Still, the interesting thing to me is the development of the universe through the coming together of time, space, and energy really isn't all that much different than what happens between us and our horses when the distance between us is correct. When that coming together within shared space is correct between us, regardless of whether or not we're working on the ground with our horse or when we're in the saddle, everything becomes effortless. It's harmony at its essence.

Today I can look back at my early days of exploration into the art of developing correct ma-ai and smile at how naïve I was as to its importance. Back then I couldn't see what the big deal was. Today, I believe it is not only one of the major keys to working with, or just being around, horses, but more importantly, I can also see that it is one of the elements that are essential to the harmony of life.

Chapter 11
Nature in Horsemanship

There is a small plaque just inside the door of our dojo. It talks of how a dojo is a microcosm for life, and how all of the skills we acquire through training as well as all the emotional ups and downs, and struggles, and triumphs that occur within the dojo walls help to prepare us for that which can happen (both good and bad) outside the dojo. Aikido training, at its core, is the development and understanding for the natural forces that surround us. When faced with a situation in which violence or discord exists or when action to preserve self is needed, aikido training allows us to blend with, connect to, and direct those forces to the most peaceful solution possible. In other words, when nature is included, harmony can be found.

I've often thought of how the same could be said for horses and horsemanship. Horses are nothing if not a study in harmony, and when I say they are a study in harmony, it's not so much that they strive to stay in harmony but rather that they are masters at reestablishing it once it has been lost. It's the way things work in nature. Without occasional discord, there can be no harmony in the first place. It is that ebb and flow that brings life, like the beating of a heart. The unfortunate thing, I think, is that over the years, we may have gotten a little sidetracked when it comes to trying to understand harmony and ultimately benefiting from the nature in horsemanship.

One of the reasons for this is that a lot of horsemanship these days isn't geared toward working with the ebb and flow that makes up harmony. It is geared toward perfection and achieving 100 percent correct responses from the horse 100 percent of the time. Now don't get me wrong here. I certainly don't see anything wrong with having high standards and working toward being the best one can be. But I also believe that anyone expecting absolute perfection from a situation that involves the interaction of two different species, such as humans and horses, is going to be in for a fairly substantial disappointment. Heck, humans don't even communicate effectively with one another 100 percent of the time, even when we speak the same language. It's no wonder we might have a little trouble getting that kind of perfection when dealing with our horses.

Besides, harmony isn't about perfection anyway. It's about synchronization and coming together for a common goal. Not the mechanical synchronization that is obtained through mindless repetition, but synchronization through a flow of blended energy between two or more individuals. It is what makes up nature, what brings the spirit to life, and ultimately, I believe it is what makes up true horsemanship.

What I'm talking about here is the type of work that strives to move beyond what one might refer to as the "synthetic horsemanship" that we see so much of these days. It's getting past the type of horsemanship where the main focus is on the human, not necessarily the horse, and where *making* the horse perform needless and often mindless tasks over

and over in the quest for "respect" is often the goal. Rather, the type of horsemanship I'm referring to here doesn't belong to anybody; it isn't trademarked, and it doesn't even have a name. It is simply the development of honest communication between horse and rider based on the best understanding we each have for one another at any given time. It's taking the good with the bad without placing blame or fault, and doing our best to direct energy instead of stifling or stopping it. In other words, getting back to the same basic concepts and principles provided by and in nature and then allowing those very same principles to shine through in our horsemanship.

Interestingly enough, however, the late comedian George Carlin once noted that the titles of the magazines we read in this country have, over the years, documented a surprising shift in our culture, and this shift may have actually worked to pull us from the "natural" roots that I'm talking about here. In 1883, when the majority of folks in the United States lived and worked in rural areas, *Life Magazine* came to be. For most of the twentieth century, *Life* was one of the nation's leading and most revered periodicals. Not only did *Life* record stories of all the historic events of the century, it also encompassed the lives of everyday people, their struggles and triumphs, as well as important natural events and disasters, and even from time to time stories on animals, both domestic and wild. It truly was a magazine about *life* from a broad and varied perspective.

In 1974 as *Life Magazine*'s readership began to slowly decline, so did that broad and varied perspective. The new magazine of the day had a title that exemplified that narrowing view. *People Magazine* began to rise in prominence, which incidentally coincided with the migration of folks from the rural areas of the country into the nation's cities. Then, in the 1980s another magazine showed up on newsstands that narrowed the perspective even more. The new magazine was called *Us*. Not to be outdone, in 2003, *Me Magazine* showed up as an online magazine.

Mr. Carlin had aptly pointed out that in just a few short years, we as a society had gone from looking at *life*, to reading *people*, to focusing on *us*, and finally we had gotten all the way down to the singularity of *me*. It may have been the cleverly orchestrated musings of a comic, but in reality, one could argue that it really isn't all that far off the mark.

Over the years, our culture here in the United States has slowly gone from one of farming, ranching, and small towns with focus on animals, neighbors, family, and community to a culture focused primarily on the fast-paced world of suburban sprawl and technological advances. Face-to-face communication within shared space has given way to impersonal correspondence through e-mail, texts, and cyber–social networking, and the ability to read and understand facial expressions and body language is being replaced by innocuous symbols at the end of a typed sentence on the screen of a computer.

In the midst of all this change is the possibility that our understanding and connection to the flow of nature that used to surround us has begun to slip through our fingers. The problem is, isolating ourselves from nature, whether intentionally or unintentionally, is not good for us. We don't do well when we lose contact with the one that brought us to the dance, and while we may find ways to tell ourselves that being isolated is okay, our subconscious will always try to find ways to bring us back into the loop.

It is my belief that one of the ways a number of people try to reconnect with nature is to either spend as much time outdoors as possible, or they turn to owning and/or working with animals. Animals are our closest connection to a time when we lived in and with nature, and research shows that just the act of touching an animal (horse, dog, cat, etc.) can lower our blood pressure and bring down stress levels. So regardless of whether we live in a high-rise in Atlanta, a townhouse in Portland, or a farmhouse in Wisconsin, many of us can't help but bring dogs, cats, or even birds into our homes, or horses into our barns. We intentionally choose to bring these animals close to us, and in living with them, it allows us the opportunity, if even at some very small level, to stay connected to nature and break loose from the singularity of modern-day life.

In the end, it would be hard to imagine where this reconnection to nature could be any more prevalent than when we spend time with horses. And, for those of us who do spend our days living, working, and learning from them, it is the horse that allows us the opportunity to listen to that beating heart, to feel that ebb and flow, and ultimately, to get back in touch with the spirit that is harmony.